Cartooning for Kids
#2

By Mike Artell

Published by MJA Creative, LLC
Copyright 2023 by Mike Artell
All rights reserved

ISBN 978-1-7324180-6-6

Printed in the U.S.A.

For additional information visit www.mikeartell.com

Table of Contents

Introduction		4
Part 1	Exaggeration	7
Part 2	Simplification	28
Part 3	Animals and Objects Doing "People" Things	41
Part 4	People in Different Poses	53
Part 5	Unusual Body Types and Gestures	65
Part 6	Monsters, Weird Creatures, and Aliens	80
Index		128

Introduction

First, think funny.

You don't have to be a great artist to be a good cartoonist, but you do have to think funny. This book will show you how to draw lots of funny people, animals, and other creatures, but it's really just a starting point. After you've learned how to draw the things in this book, try to come up with your own ideas for cartoon characters and situations.

How do you do that? By paying attention to what's going on around you. During the day, you may hear people say funny things or you might see a funny situation that someone has gotten into. When that happens, write it down. Many of the world's greatest songs and inventions came to people when they were doing something else. Fortunately for us, those people made a note of their wonderful ideas right away. You'll get great ideas too, so always keep some paper and a pencil nearby.

You can usually make a funny scene by changing something small about a common situation. For example, it's not unusual to have a new neighbor move in next door to you. But what if that neighbor is from another planet? Or what if the new neighbors are a family of giants? Or talking cows? Get the idea? If you change just one thing, you can come up with lots of funny ideas.

Remember, cartoonists have to THINK funny. The drawing skills are secondary to the humor. Even if you're the world's greatest illustrator, you won't be a good *cartoonist* unless you first THINK funny.

I hope you enjoy this book and that it teaches you skills you can use for the rest of your life. Have fun!

Mike Artell

Materials You'll Need

One of the nice things about cartooning is that it requires very few materials. In fact, all you really need is a pencil and some paper. Here are some additional materials you might want to have on hand:

A soft, rubber eraser
Erasers that are soft and flexible usually seem to erase more cleanly. You might want to try using different kinds of erasers to see which you prefer.

Black drawing pencils
Your art supply store can help you choose drawing pencils that are just right for shading as well as drawing. Soft leads can be smudged to create shadows and shading. Harder leads are best when you are drawing lots of detail.

Colored pencils
There are many kinds of colored pencils. Some are soft and create a thick, smooth line. Others are harder and are best when you need a thin, precise line. Softer colored pencils can be blended to produce combinations of colors. There's even a colorless "blending" pencil that you can buy for just that purpose. Once again, your art supply store can help you choose which colored pencils are best for your style of cartooning.

Markers
Chances are you've already done a lot of drawing and coloring with water-based markers. Markers come in an endless variety of colors. You'll need some basic colors, but it's also a good idea to buy some pastels and bold markers, as well as some markers for different skin tones. Alcohol-based markers often "bleed" through the paper and stain your hands, so it's better to use water-based markers. Start a collection of markers and keep them in a plastic container with a tight lid to help keep them from drying up.

Pens

Try drawing in pencil first. When you're satisfied with the way your drawing looks, put it on a light table, cover it with a clean piece of paper, and trace your pencil drawing in ink. Like markers, there are many kinds of pens. Which pen you use is really up to you. Thin fiber-tipped pens usually work well, but occasionally a steel-tipped technical pen is good, too. It just depends on what you're drawing. Black is the most common color, but some wonderful new gel pens offer rich, bright colors that are a lot of fun. Experiment with different pens until you find the one you like best.

Paint

Watercolors are easy to work with and their colors are wonderful. Watercolors also blend together beautifully. Like any paint, watercolors can be a little messy. You'll need some room to spread out as you work, so keep that in mind before you start. Watercolors also take time to dry. You can speed things up by using a hair dryer to dry each section of your painting as you finish it.

Paper

It's always a good idea to make your rough sketch on the same size paper as your final cartoon. Some common paper sizes are 8½″ x 11″ or 9″ x 12″. Try doing the "rough" cartoons on plain white copier paper and then tracing your designs onto a coated paper with a slick surface. Coated paper can be found at your local print shop. The slick surface makes a very clean black line.

If you're planning to use watercolors or markers, try tracing your drawings onto smooth watercolor paper. Bristol board is a good substitute if you want a heavier paper. If you browse through the papers in your local art supply store, you'll find different weights, colors, and even patterns. Experimenting with different papers is the best way to find what works for you. The people at the store can tell you which papers work best with different pencils, markers, and paints.

Part I
Exaggeration

Cartoons are different from "regular" illustrations in one important way: Cartoons are always meant to make the reader smile. Some people would say that superhero comic book cartoons don't always make the reader smile, and that's true. But I don't think of superhero comic book images as "cartoons"; I think of them as illustrations. In superhero comic books (or graphic novels), the characters often have muscles and facial features that are very realistic. I think true cartoons are exaggerations and simplifications of the way people really look.

If you compare the illustrations in a superhero comic book or graphic novel with the cartoons on the comics page in your local newspaper, you'll see what I mean. Usually the characters on the comics page have big noses or crazy eyes or some physical feature that makes them look funny. Also, their hair might stand up or their eyes might pop out of their heads when they get scared. You won't see those traits very often in a superhero comic.

One of the best ways to make your drawings look "cartoony" is to exaggerate something about the character or situation.

Here are some examples. Look at this illustration of a girl.

She looks pretty normal, doesn't she? Now, let's change some of her facial features. . . .

Here's the same girl with an exaggerated mouth and teeth.

She looks a little stranger now, doesn't she?

Now let's exaggerate her eyes and nose . . . or her hair . . .

Can you see how exaggeration makes normal illustrations look very cartoony? Try it yourself. Draw a normal-looking person. Then draw the person again, but exaggerate one or two or your character's facial features.

One of the best ways to exaggerate something is to draw it BIG. You may want to draw cartoon characters that are big like giants or characters with big hair or muscles. Or you may just want to draw a character who is very heavy. Let's practice drawing some big people.

Draw an egg-shaped head and a big U-shaped nose. Make the neck thick and short.

From the neck, go out to each side and draw shoulders. Add arms and a square stomach.

Add some simple hands at his side.

Remember... when it comes to drawing **BIG** people... **THICK** is the trick!

Now draw the legs. They should be thick and not too long. Add wide feet.

You've just drawn a basic "big" person. Of course, you can always use some exaggeration to make the character's nose, mouth, or eyes bigger. You can also try making the neck or legs VERY thick. Experiment a little with the characters you like to draw. First draw them the way you would normally draw them. Then draw them again with much thicker necks, bodies, and legs.

Now let's draw a REALLY big person—a GIANT.

If you were looking up at a giant, his head would look small. That's because things look smaller when they're farther away from us. So let's start with a small head for this giant.

 It looks really small, doesn't it? That's OK. It's supposed to be small.

Now add a shirt and big, thick hands. Notice the shading on the shirt and the hair on the hands. Adding little details like these makes your drawing look a lot better.

Draw some thick legs and big boots to complete your giant. Then try drawing different kinds of backgrounds behind him. On the previous page, the giant was standing in front of a mountain. Where else could you put him?

You can also draw big animals. For example, here's a quick way to draw a whale.

Begin with a curvy line for the body.

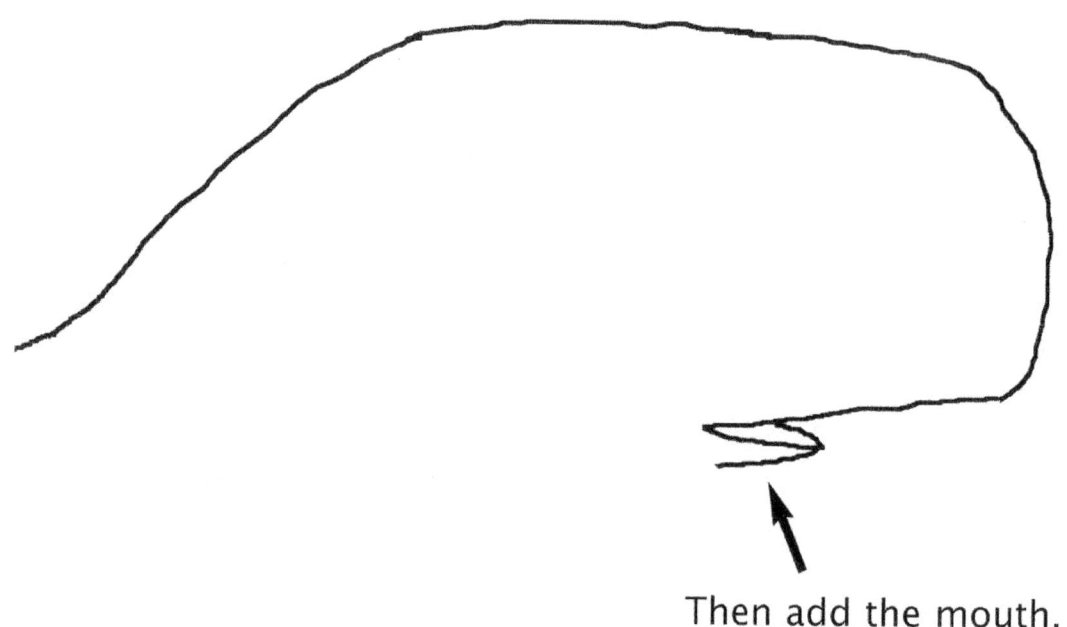

Then add the mouth.

Next, add the bottom of the whale and a tail, like this...

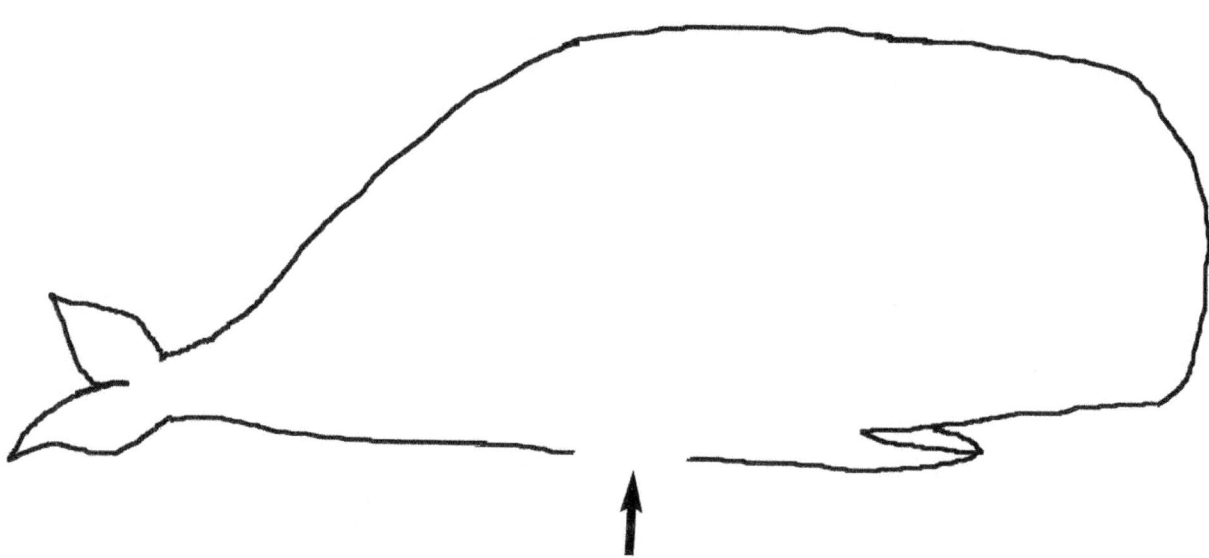

Leave a little space open at the bottom.

Draw a fin on the bottom of the body and a hole in the top of the whale's head. You can also color in the inside of the whale's mouth. Don't forget to add an eye.

Thar' She Blows!!

Here's one way to draw a giant turtle.

Draw a shell.

Add a head and neck. Draw the front of the face very flat.

Now give your turtle some big, thick legs.

Add a tail. Draw markings on the shell, scales on the legs, and wrinkles on the neck.

16

Now, let's draw a giraffe.

Begin by drawing these lines.

Add eyes and horns.

Giraffes have big ears and large nostrils.

All that's left are some spots on the neck and shading inside the ears.

HEY! Where's the rest of the giraffe?

Sometimes, it's fun to draw only PART of an animal. Then you can "hide" the animal in water or behind some trees. Try drawing an animal you draw often. This time, draw just the head and neck of the animal. Make sure to draw the head and neck BIG!

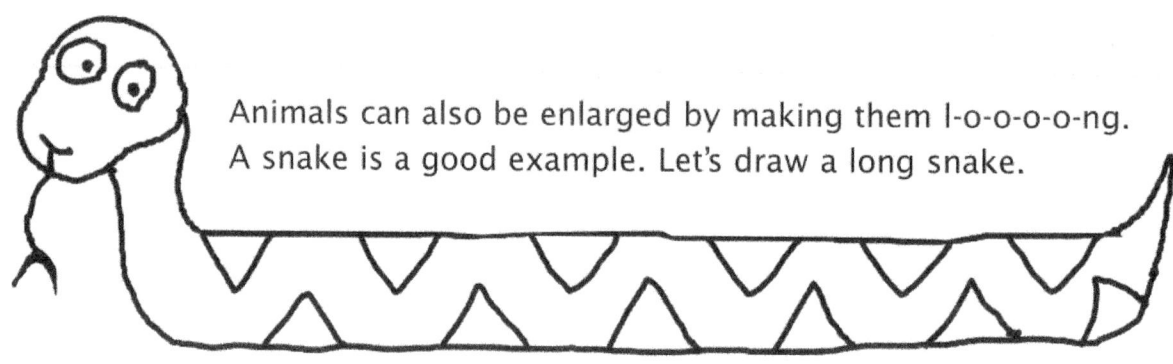

Animals can also be enlarged by making them l-o-o-o-o-ng. A snake is a good example. Let's draw a long snake.

Begin by drawing the head and tongue.

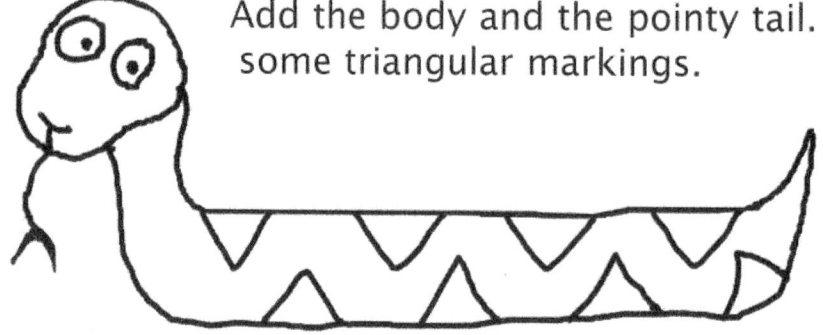

Add the body and the pointy tail. Don't forget some triangular markings.

The longer you make your snake, the funnier it will be. This snake is a little longer.

This snake is SERIOUSLY long. And it's funnier than either of the other two snakes, isn't it?

You can also take normal animals and make them look funnier if you just exaggerate one or more of their body parts. This cow is a good example. Let's draw it.

This alligator has an exaggerated head.

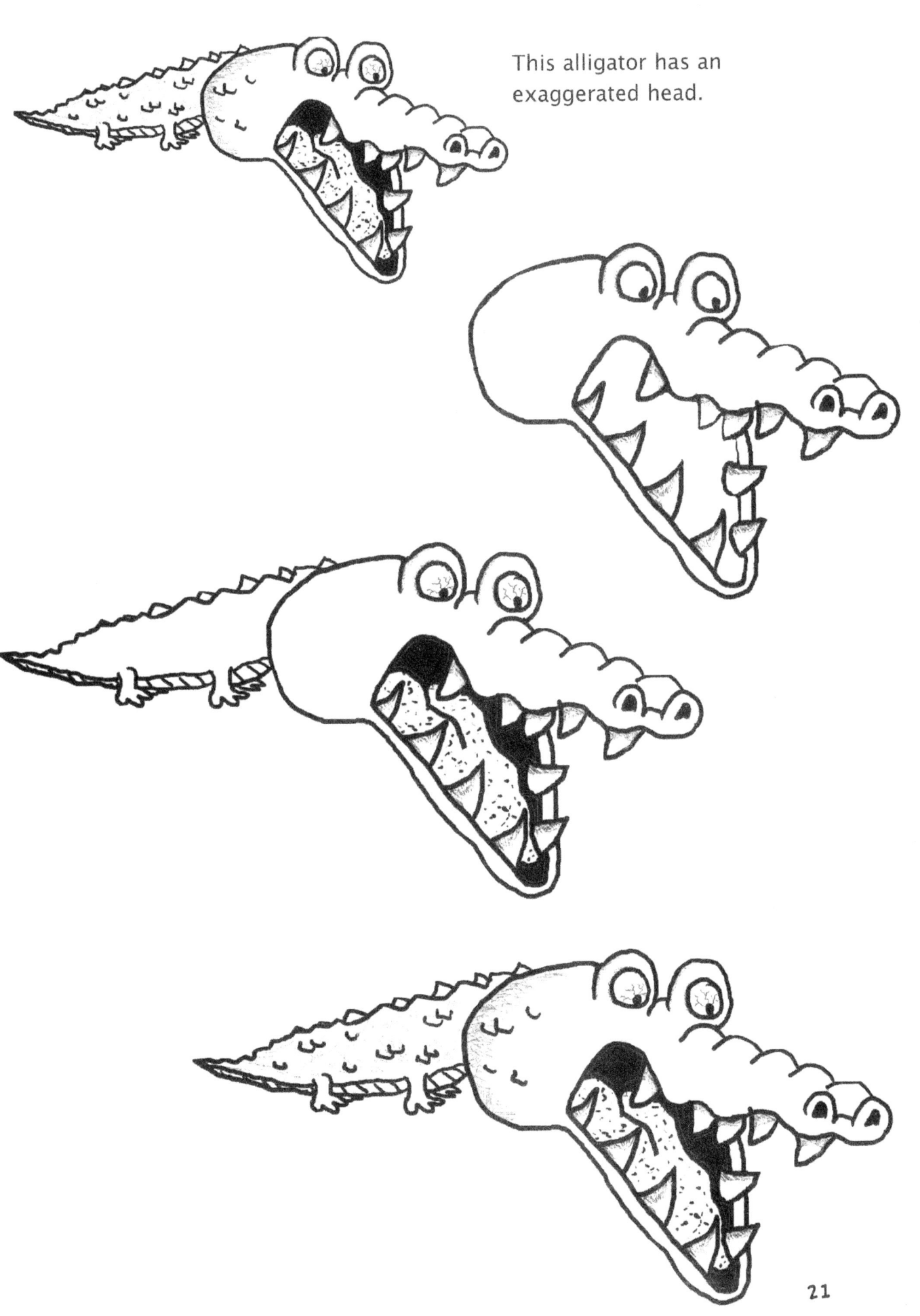

Here are some more ideas for weird animal bodies.

Tall, skinny mouse

Hummingbird with extra-long beak

Spider with incredibly long legs

Here's a frog to draw. After you've drawn it, think about what you could do to make it funny. Could you make the eyes HUGE? Could you make the legs bigger? What could you do with the mouth to make this drawing more amusing?

Think about animals that are known for some physical characteristic. Giraffes are known for their long necks. Sharks are known for their teeth. Beavers are known for their flat tails. Peacocks are known for their brightly colored feathers.

How could you change an animal's special characteristic to make it funny? What could you do to a giraffe's neck (or spots)? What could you change about a shark to add some humor to your drawing? Could you draw a beaver's tail bigger, smaller, weirder? How could you draw a peacock's feathers in an unusual or outrageous way?

Try drawing some strange animals of your own on another sheet of paper.

Another way to exaggerate is by drawing people many times. Here are some examples of how repeating drawings of people can be funny.

This dad has a small problem. His baby is crying.

This dad has a much bigger problem. The babies are basically the same, but some minor changes have been made to their facial expressions and hair. And of course, there's one baby who has had a little "accident."

This is a good example of how you can exaggerate by repeating.

Try drawing one person. Then draw the same person over and over with some minor changes to his or her hair and facial features.

This guy is about to enjoy a piece of cake, which his friend sure would like to share with him.

Our character doesn't mind sharing with his best friend. After all, it's just one other person, right?

But you can make the situation much funnier if you draw a crowd of people.

You can also use repetition when you draw animals. Here are some ideas for you to try.

This little dog is happy because he found a bone. Let's draw this dog.

First draw a smiling dog face.

Add a head and ears. Then add a round body and one arm.

Don't finish the other arm yet.

Add a tail, legs, and a hand holding a bone, and you're all done!

If we use repetition to exaggerate the number of bones, we get a much funnier picture. Now our little dog is REALLY happy.

Remember, you can make your drawings funnier if you use exaggeration. You can exaggerate by making things big, by making them long, or by repeating elements of the drawing many times. Take some time to think of ways you could add these exaggeration techniques to things you like to draw. Make small things big. Make big things gigantic. Make normal things long. Make long things incredibly long. Look for one object or character in your drawing and draw it over and over again, changing it just a little bit each time. When you learn these techniques, you'll be amazed at how funny your cartoons become.

Part 2

Simplification

Exaggeration is a handy way to change typical drawings into great cartoons. Another technique that cartoonists use is simplification. Simplification simply means, "Don't draw TOO MUCH." Keep it basic. There are times when you want to draw lots of detail, but there are many more times when it makes sense to simplify your drawings. Here are some examples of simplified drawings.

Here's a man's face with lots of detail.

Here's a simplified version of the same face. This face looks more cartoony, doesn't it?

Now look at the two girls in the drawings below. Simplifying makes the girl on the right look like a cartoon.

It's a good idea (and a lot of fun!) to experiment with different simplified facial features to see which work best on your cartoon characters. Let's try experimenting with the facial features in this drawing.

Begin by drawing this woman's head and hair. Add some earrings, too.

Now add a neck and a shirt. Notice that you don't have to draw the entire shirt. Just draw the shoulders and collar.

Here's where you start experimenting.

Instead of drawing these eyes, which have a lot of detail,

try drawing these simplified eyes on the woman's face.

Instead of drawing this mouth,

try drawing one of these mouths.

And you can replace this nose . . .

with one of these.

There are times when you want to include lots of details in your drawings, but you don't usually need to add too many facial details to cartoon people. In fact, the reason many people don't think they draw cartoons well is because they try to draw too much detail.

On another sheet of paper, draw each of the heads below, several times. Then draw different combinations of simplified eyes, noses, and mouths on each head. If you like, you can add mustaches or eyeglasses to your characters to make them funnier.

You can also simplify animals. Here's a very detailed drawing of a parrot. This parrot has many different kinds of feathers. Some are long and pointy, while others are rounded and soft. The parrot's eye is large for its head.

Now here's a simplified, cartoony version of the same parrot. This parrot has eyes like a human. The feathers have been simplified. Even though this drawing doesn't look like a real parrot, we can tell what kind of animal it is and we have given it some personality.

Let's draw the cartoon parrot.

Begin with a beak and two "human" eyes.

Add feathers around the head.

Add feathers on the back and side.

Finish by adding front feathers, a foot, and a simple branch. TA-DA! You did it!

Here's a quick sketch of a baby elephant. It looks pretty good, but it's not funny. Let's simplify it.

This little elephant may not look as "real" as the first elephant, but he's a lot more fun.

Let's draw this little guy.

Begin by drawing the eyes, nose, and mouth.

Add lines on the nose and some big, floppy ears.

Next, draw a round body. Leave a little space at the bottom for the right front leg. Add a tail, too.

Now all you have to do is draw some legs and toenails to complete your baby elephant!

Simplified Gestures

A gesture is a movement you make with your arms, face, or other part of your body. Gestures are used to express a thought or an emotion or to get someone's attention. Here are some simple gestures you can draw.

Let's draw this "groovy" hippie.

Start with a fuzzy beard, wild hair, and little round glasses.

Add a shirt, vest, and arms. Make one hand do the "peace" sign.

Draw the bottom of the shirt, some pants, and bare feet. You can add a happy face on the shirt, a shadow on the ground, or anything else you think might make your drawing look better.

This gesture means, "Be quiet!" Usually we make a "shhhh" sound when we make this gesture.

These fingers are pointing "That way" . . . and "Up."

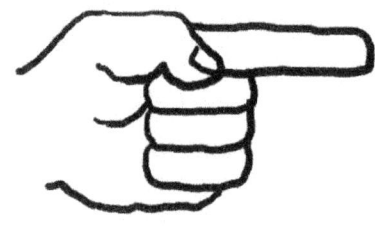 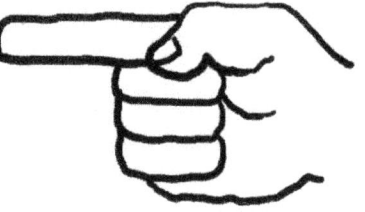 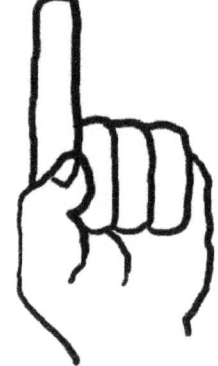

This gesture means, "OK" or "Good."

When you make a wish, you make this gesture.

And this guy wants us to
STOP!!

We make gestures with our faces, too. Here are some facial gestures you can draw. Try to imagine what each character is thinking.

Part 3
Animals and Objects Doing "People" Things

One way to make your animal drawings funnier is to have the animals do things that people do. Here are some drawings of animals doing things that you normally only see people doing.

Can you imagine a cat driving a car? Just the idea is funny. In this drawing, the steering wheel and the seat are much larger than the cat, which makes the cat look smaller. It's also funny to simplify the cat's eyes so it looks like the cat is staring at the road and concentrating very hard.

It's even funnier if you add some mice to help our cat drive.

Here's something you don't see every day . . . an elephant playing a video game. Like the cat on the previous page, the elephant's eyes are "glued" to what it is watching. If we stick its tongue out, the elephant looks like it's trying really hard to win the game. Also notice how the elephant's legs extend backward to make it look like it's lying on its stomach.

You don't have to draw animals parachuting out of airplanes or performing any other "fantastic" feats. It's actually funnier if you draw them doing ordinary, everyday things.

Here are some more funny animal situations you can draw:

- A dinosaur ice skating
- A shark cooking dinner
- An octopus playing a guitar
- A worm reading a book
- A hippo building a house
- An eagle working out in the gym
- A rhinoceros mowing the lawn
- A beaver at the dentist's office
- A pig in a school desk
- A giraffe grocery shopping
- A dog talking on a cell phone
- A hamster planting a garden
- A duck doing the weather report on TV

You can also give your cartoon animals human emotions. It's funny when an animal's eyes open up and its mouth drops. It's also funny when an animal laughs like a human.

Here are some examples of animals showing human facial expressions. Draw these and then try some of your own animals with similar expressions.

This bear is shocked! Notice how its eyes are open wide and the lower half of its mouth has dropped down. The bear's eyebrows are also higher than normal. This expression can be used to show surprise and even mild fear. Draw the bear with this expression. Then draw the bear again, but exaggerate the expression. You could make his eyes even bigger or make his eyebrows pop off his head. Try dropping his mouth w-a-a-a-a-y down on his face.

Remember, cartoonists have to be able to **THINK FUNNY**. Try to think of some funny situation that would cause the bear to look this way. Could it be that he just walked into his house and saw Goldilocks? Or perhaps a swarm of bees is headed in his direction?

 This fish is angry. The top of its eye is a straight line and the bottom of its eye is curved. This is always a good way to show angry eyes. The mouth is also turned down. Notice the little "special effect" of bubbles. They show that the fish is underwater.

Try drawing this fish with the expression it has now, and then draw the fish again with an exaggerated expression.

Below are animals with some other expressions you can play with. Try drawing each of the animals below with exaggerated expressions. Have fun and remember to use your sense of humor.

Bored pig

Laughing alligator

Bee in love

46

We know that it's funny to draw animals doing "people" things like driving a car or playing video games, but you can also draw objects doing people things. Look at these cartoons.

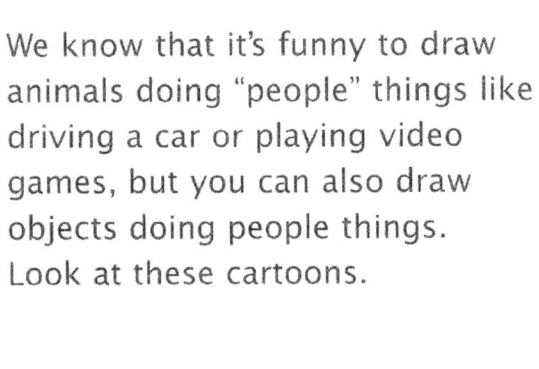

A book picking a flower

A pencil thinking

A house waving a flag

On another sheet of paper, draw the computer and mailbox below.
Then make each of them do something that a human being would do.

Eyes are the most important facial feature when it comes to showing emotions. There are an unlimited number of eye shapes and sizes. Here are a few.

Angry, fierce, scary

Sweet, innocent

Worried, scared, in pain

Suspicious, sneaky

Bored, tired, sleepy

Wacky, crazy

Confused, freaked out

Smiling, sweet, friendly

Jolly, happy

Draw this flower on another sheet of paper. Then experiment with different eyes to see which work best for the emotion you want to show.

Mouths also help show emotions. Draw the baseball bat below on another sheet of paper. Add eyes, and then draw one of these mouths.

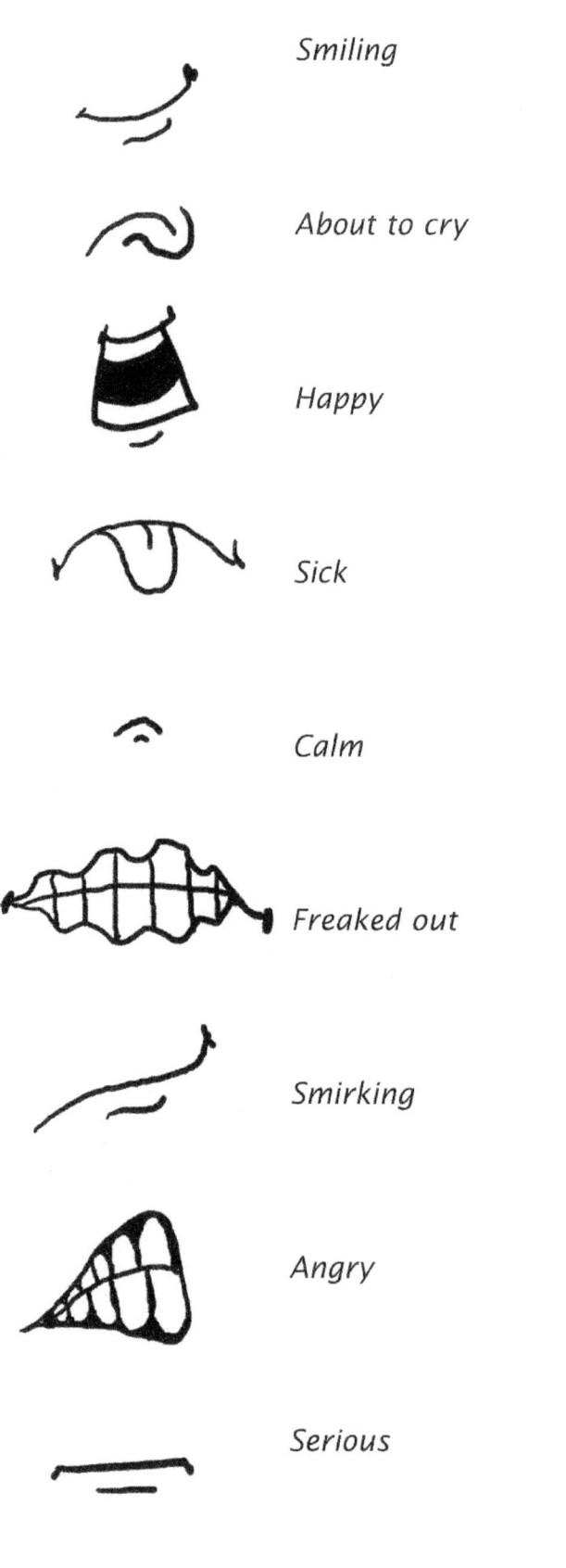

Smiling

About to cry

Happy

Sick

Calm

Freaked out

Smirking

Angry

Serious

One way to make your drawings funnier is to draw the opposite of what you would expect or what is typical. Look at these examples of drawing opposites.

Here's a tiger cub that prefers vegetables to meat.

Mosquitoes are always biting people. Wouldn't it be funny if we turned the tables and let a human bite a mosquito?

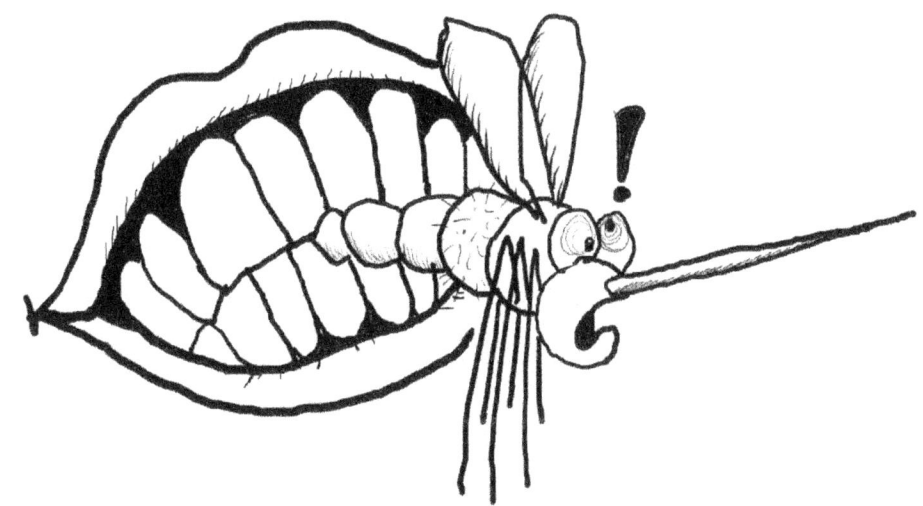

How about a trash can that wants to smell nice?

Try drawing some of these "opposite" ideas:

    A polar bear that doesn't like cold weather

    A superhero that is wimpy

    A tortoise that can run very fast

    A bat that is afraid of the dark

    A soccer ball that kicks back when it is kicked

Part 4
People in Different Poses

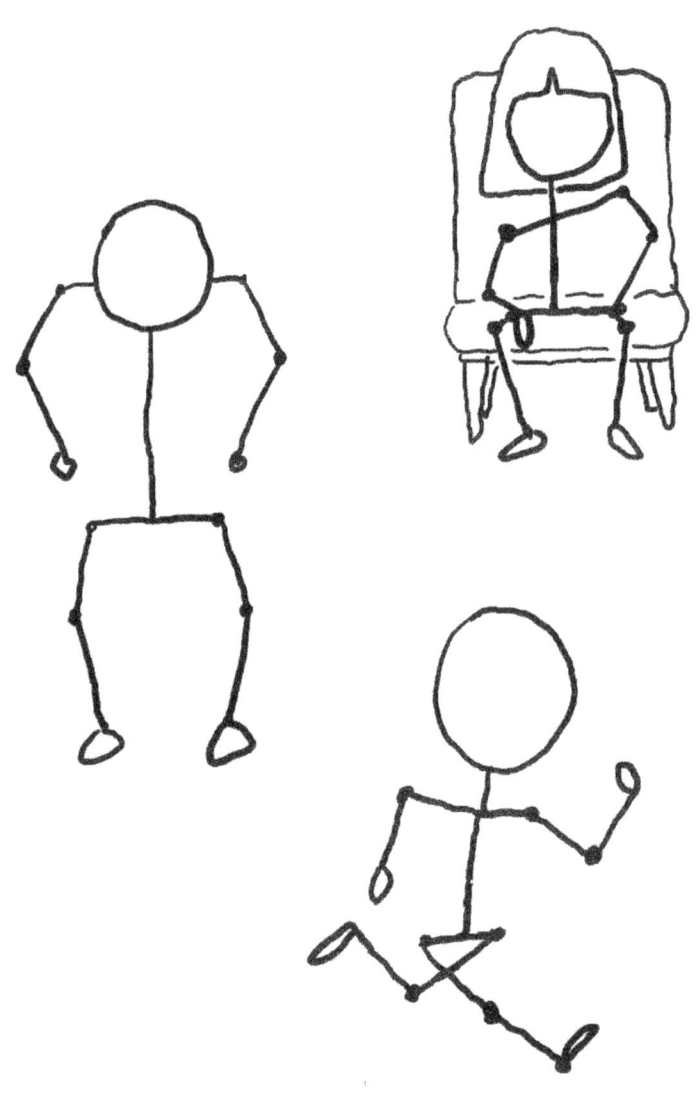

Sometimes young cartoonists find it hard to draw people standing—especially from a side view. Here are some tips for drawing people standing in different poses.

Lots of young cartoonists draw people standing this way. But there's something wrong with this picture. Look at the girl's feet: One foot points to the left and one foot to the right, which is not how people usually stand.

The feet on this girl look much more natural. They're pointing toward us.

Watch real people on the street, at your school, or at the mall. Notice which way their feet point when they walk toward you or when they're facing you.

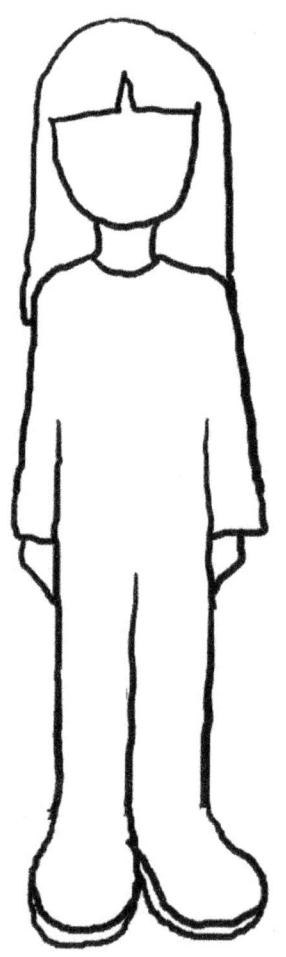

54

Here are some cartoons of people standing. Try to draw them.

You can see just a little bit of this boy's left shoulder and sleeve. Your view of the boy's left hand is blocked by his body.

Now look at this boy's feet. You can see that his left shoe is a little higher up in the picture than the right shoe. And you can see the toe of the left shoe, but not the heel.

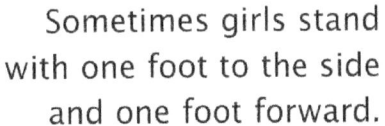
Sometimes girls stand with one foot to the side and one foot forward.

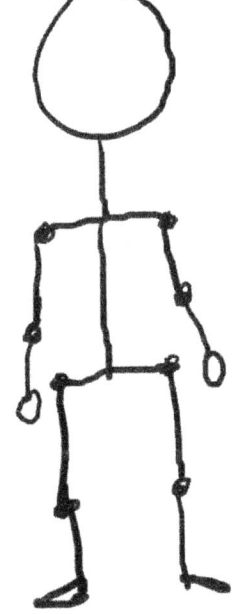

Most people think that stick men aren't real cartoons. But stick men can be very helpful when you're trying to draw people in unusual positions.

On the next few pages we'll use stick men to help us understand how people bend and move.

Standing

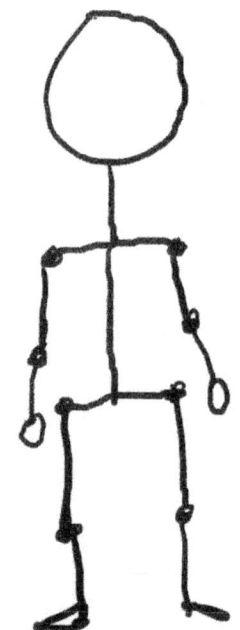

Draw a stick man. Add dots at each of the main joints of the body.

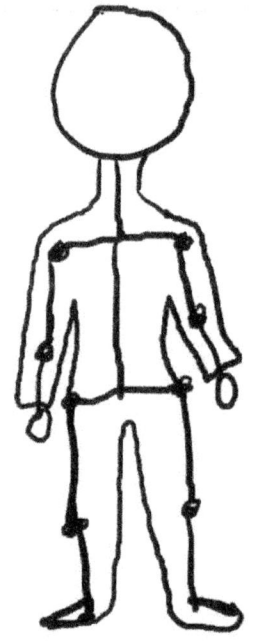

Now draw around the basic stick man shape to add fullness to your character.

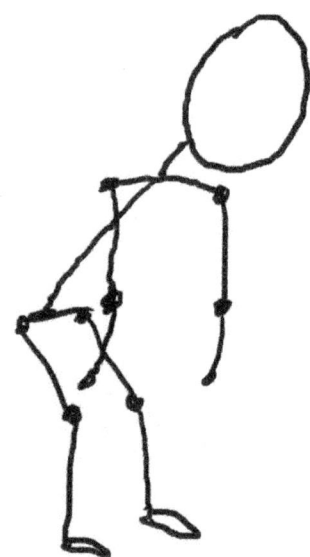

Try bending your stick man along the joints of his body. Here's how to make a stick man bend over.

Now add fullness to the stick man's body and erase the basic stick man shape.

Here are some more stick men in various poses. Try drawing them and then add fullness to their bodies to make them look more real.

Confused, thinking, wondering

Waving hello or good-bye, raising a hand to answer a question

Crouching down, "ducking," acting timid or shy

Doing a handstand

Jumping, cheering

If you draw this character with angry facial features and with his fists clenched, he will look very angry. If you draw him with a silly face, hands open, and palms pointing forward, he will look like he's clueless or saying, "I don't know."

Sitting

We've been drawing stick men. Now let's draw some stick women. Stick women can come in very handy when you want to draw cartoon characters sitting down. Here are some sitting stick women you can practice drawing.

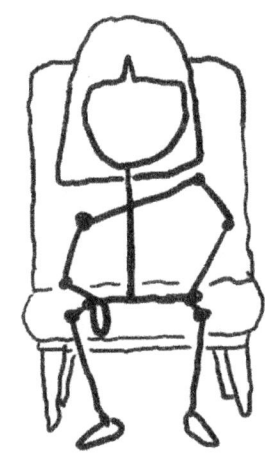

This stick woman is sitting on a chair. Notice how the line of her shoulders is slanted. Also notice how the lines from her hips to her knees are very short. That's because her legs are pointing toward us. They look shorter because of the angle at which we see them.

This stick woman is sitting on a stool. We're looking at her from the side, so we really can't see the line of her shoulders or hips. In fact, the shoulders and hips are just dots. Notice that the line from her hips to her knees goes up on an angle. The lower the stool, the greater the angle. If the stool were very low, the hips would be low, too, and the knees would be very high.

This stick woman is lying on the ground with her left arm on her knee. You can find lots of images of people sitting and lying down in newspapers and in magazines. Cut out some of those pictures and try to draw a stick person over the image to see where the joints bend. This will help you when you draw your own characters.

Walking and Running

This stick man is walking. The right leg and the left arm are forward. The left leg and the right arm are back.

This stick man is walking faster. The arms and legs stretch farther forward and back.

This stick man is running.

If we add muscles, skin, hair, and clothes to the "running" stick man, we may get a character that looks like this.

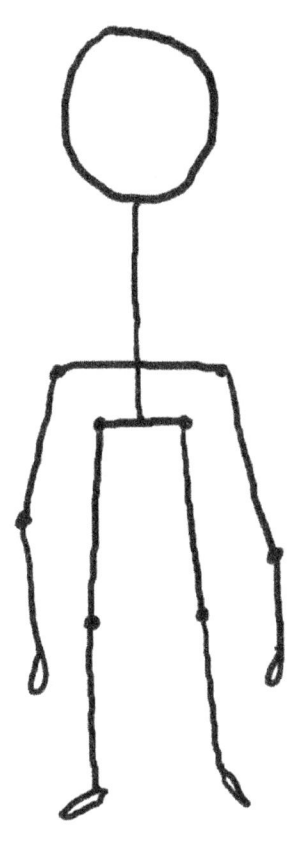

You can have some fun if you stretch and shrink different joint connections of your cartoon characters.

This stick man has extra-long arms and a long neck.

Here's the same stick man, "fleshed out" with skin, hair, clothes, and facial features. Weird!

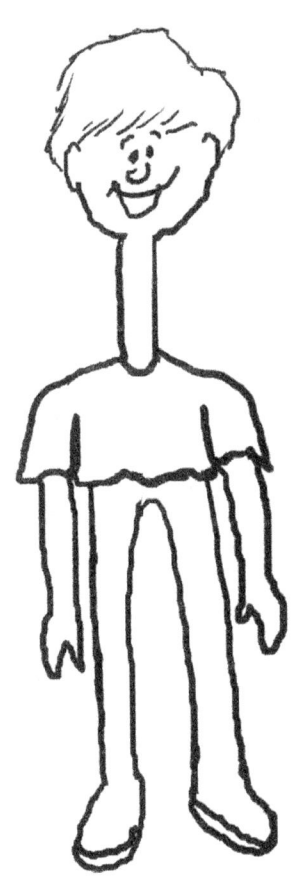

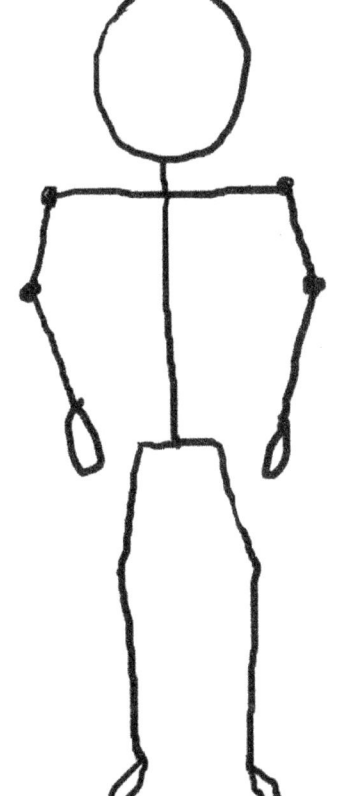

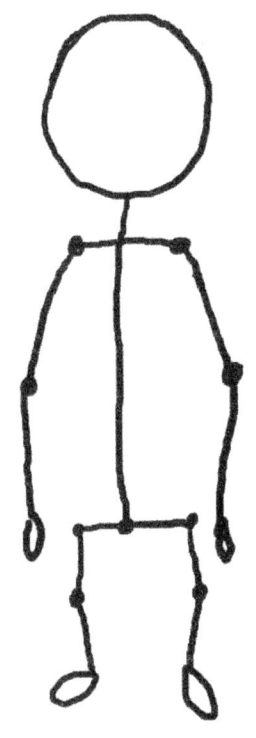

On another sheet of paper, try "fleshing out" these two weird stick men.

Slipping

Look how both arms and one leg are bent backward, while the other leg is bent forward. The curved lines around this man's elbow, knee, and foot show movement.

Falling

This man is falling headfirst and has one arm up near his face. The vertical lines cutting through the curved "movement" lines show the direction from which this man is falling.

This girl is trying to balance on one leg. Look at the foot that's on the ground. Now follow it up to her leg, hips, chest, and arm. Can you see that it's almost a straight line from her foot all the way up to the point where her arm bends over her head?

Here are some more stick figure poses for you to try:

Shooting a basketball jump shot

Riding a skateboard

Pushing a lawnmower

Doing a back flip off a diving board

Pulling a wagon

Doing a pushup

Holding a sign on a stick

Kicking a soccer ball

Hanging upside down from a tree branch

Part 5
Unusual Body Types and Gestures

Body Shapes

Bodies are as different as faces. Some people are tall and thin, while others are short and heavy. Most of us are somewhere in between. By changing the shape of your cartoon characters' bodies, you can add a lot of fun to what you're drawing.

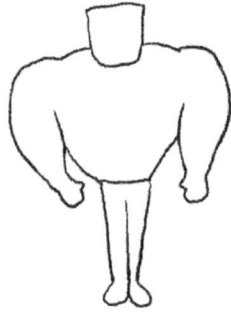

The superhero body has a square head, a triangular chest, and small hips. The body also has large arms and small hands.

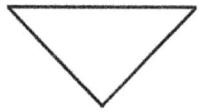

Notice the triangle-shaped chest.

Draw the superhero body in three steps.

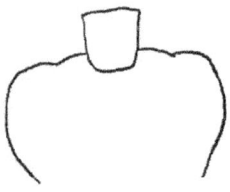 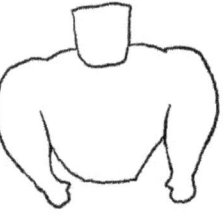 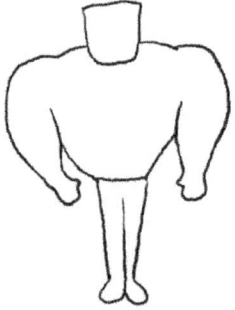

This is a gourd.

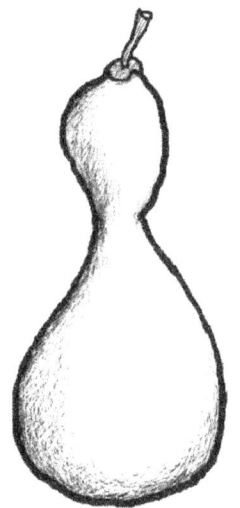

Sometimes, people are shaped like gourds.

Draw the gourd body in three steps.

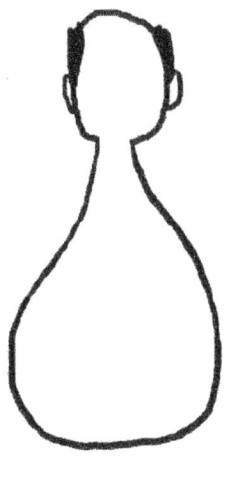 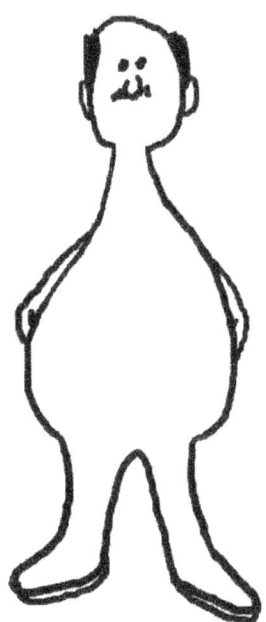 

Square body

Oval body

Rectangular body

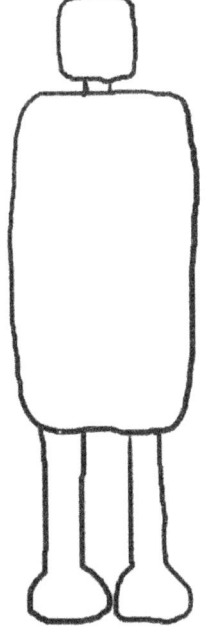

Try drawing bodies in the shapes of vegetables, fruits, nuts, and other food items. Look around your house or yard for items that could be body shapes. Kitchen or bathroom items might give you some ideas, too.

Does your family have a "junk drawer"? If so, look in there and see if there are some objects that could serve as models for people's bodies. Remember—the idea is to think funny.

Talking

When you draw your cartoon characters talking, concentrate on what happens to their eyes, eyebrows, and mouths. That's where the emotion is.

This little girl looks up as she talks. Her mouth is small and is shaped like a rounded triangle.

This girl is older. Her eyes are closed as she talks to a friend on the phone. Notice her eyebrows. What do you think she's saying?

This boy is whispering something to a friend.

These two ball players are shouting.

Here are some more ways to show people talking. Stand in front of a mirror and watch what happens when you talk in different ways. Sometimes your mouth will shift to one side of your face, or it might open wide. This exercise will give you ideas you can use when you draw your cartoons.

On another sheet of paper, draw the people below and make them talk. Experiment with different mouths, eyes, and eyebrows.

Here are some common things you see people doing every day. Pay attention to the way the bodies, arms, legs, and faces look. Try drawing people doing some everyday actions.

Girl doing homework

Boy eating a hamburger

Here are some more everyday actions for you to draw. Remember to use your stick people to put the arms, legs, and bodies in the right positions.

An old lady walking her dog
A man fishing
A very young girl kicking a ball
A girl flying a kite
A lady holding a potted plant
A man typing on a computer
A boy climbing a wooden fence
A girl looking out her bedroom window
A baby reading a book
A girl sitting in a tree
An old man playing a guitar

If it helps, have friends or family act as your models. Ask them to do an everyday action and then draw them as they do it.

Hair

Hair can make a huge difference in the appearance of your cartoon characters. You can draw hair short, long, straight, curly—almost any way you'd like. Look at the faces below. The first face has no hair. Draw the basic boy face on another sheet of paper. Now pick one of the other faces and add that kind of hair to the face you just drew. Draw the face again. Now draw a different kind of hair. After you've practiced drawing the examples below, try drawing some of your own hairstyles. You can look in a magazine, a newspaper, or on TV for ideas.

Basic boy face

Hair doesn't have to be boring. Try drawing the basic face again. This time add some WILD hair!

Now let's have some fun with girl's hair. We'll start the same way. On another sheet of paper, draw the face on the left. After you've drawn the face, add one of the hairstyles you see below. Then draw the face again and try a different hairstyle on your cartoon character. Experiment with your own hairstyle ideas, too.

These hairstyles look fairly normal. But you can have some fun by giving your cartoon girls some OUTRAGEOUS hair. Let's give it a try.

77

On another sheet of paper, draw the basic girl face. Then add one of these hairstyles or draw one of your own.

Basic girl face

You don't expect to see wild, crazy hair on old people or on babies. That's why it's funny when you do see it. It's surprising. Look at this old man and this little baby. Have you ever seen people their age with hair like this?

Think about other people you could give wild, crazy hair to. Or try taking hair away from people who usually have it. Sometimes bald characters are as funny as those who have hair.

Part 6

Monsters, Weird Creatures, and Aliens

Monsters aren't so scary if you draw them in a funny way. Let's experiment with some famous monster characters.

Here's the most famous monster of all . . .

FRANKENSTEIN!

Happy Frankie

Angry Frankie

Sleepy Frankie

Frankie in love

Sad Frankie

Cool Frankie

He howls at the full moon. He's . . . # WOLFMAN!

First draw angry eyes, a pig nose, and pointy teeth.

Then add lots of hair and sideburns. Give your character a pointy chin and heavy eyebrows.

Add long, hairy fingers. Then put it all on a normal body.

If there's a Wolf Man, there should also be a Wolf Woman. And maybe they have a Wolf Baby. Here they are!

On another sheet of paper, try drawing other Wolf characters. Here are some ideas.

Wolf Grandma

Wolf Grandpa

Wolf Teenager

Wolf Neighbor

Wolf Postman

Wolf Goldfish

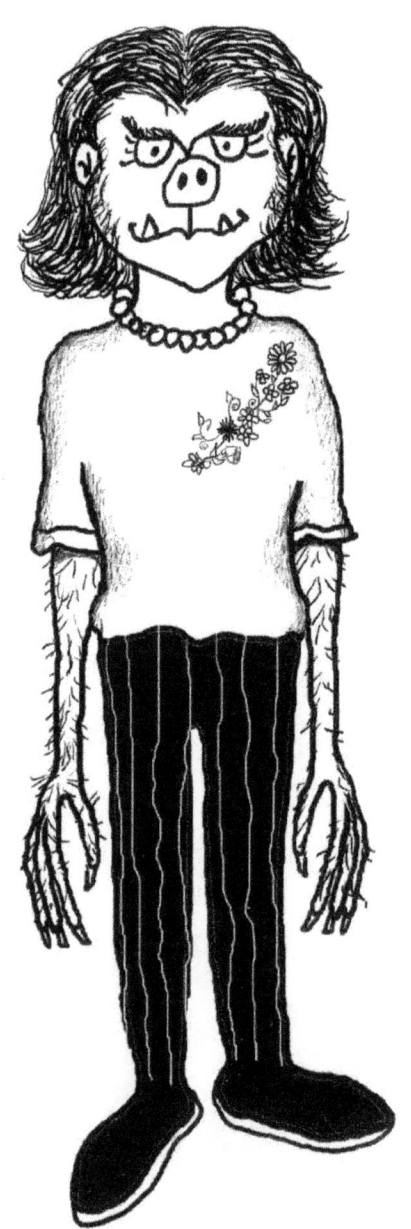

All you have to do is draw a normal human or animal body and then add the basic wolf face and long fingers.

I want my **MUMMY!**

Mummies are easy to draw because you really only have to draw the outline of the character.

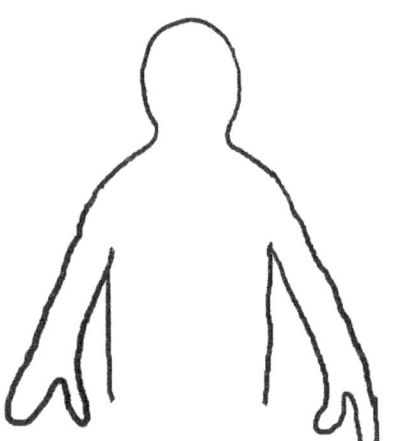

Draw the head, arms, and chest of this mummy.

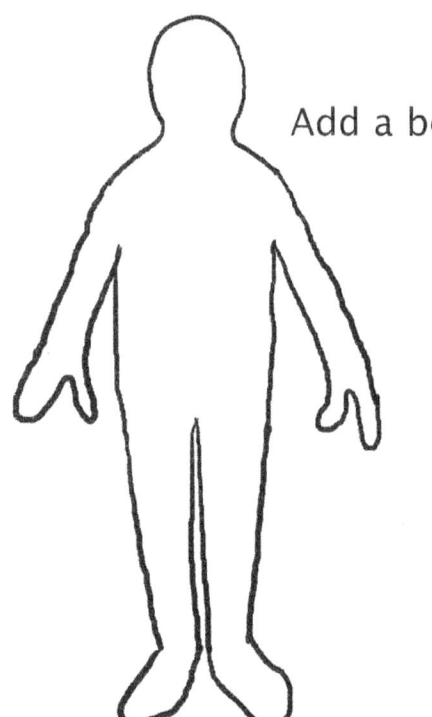

Add a body.

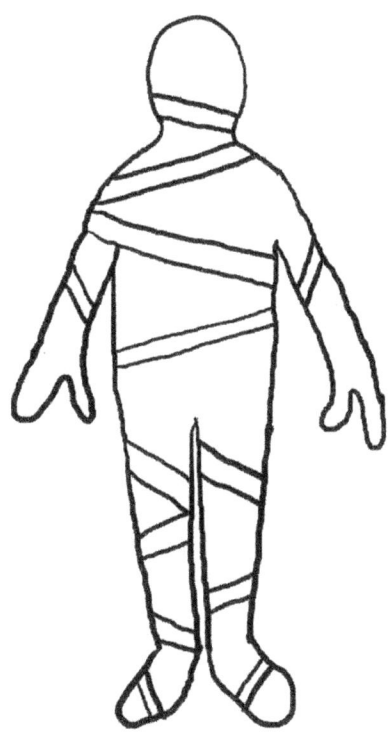

Now start drawing the cloth in which the mummy is wrapped. It's a good idea to use a Z-shaped pattern when you draw the mummy's bandages.

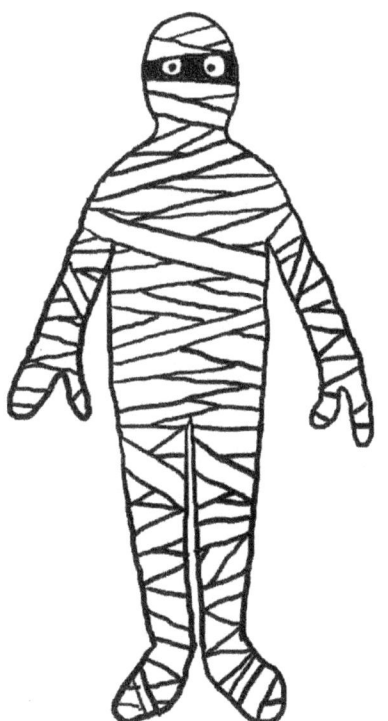

Leave a rectangular area for the eyes and darken them in.

85

Your mummies don't have to be people. They can be animals, too. Here's how to draw a mummy dog. Start by drawing the outline of the dog, like this:

Add the crisscross cloth. Because dogs walk on all fours, most of the cloth should be drawn with up and down diagonal lines rather than with side-to-side diagonal lines. Don't forget to leave a space for your mummy dog's eyes.

On another sheet of paper, draw these animal outlines and then add diagonal cloth to make them look like mummies. After you do that, try to think of other animals that you could "mummify."

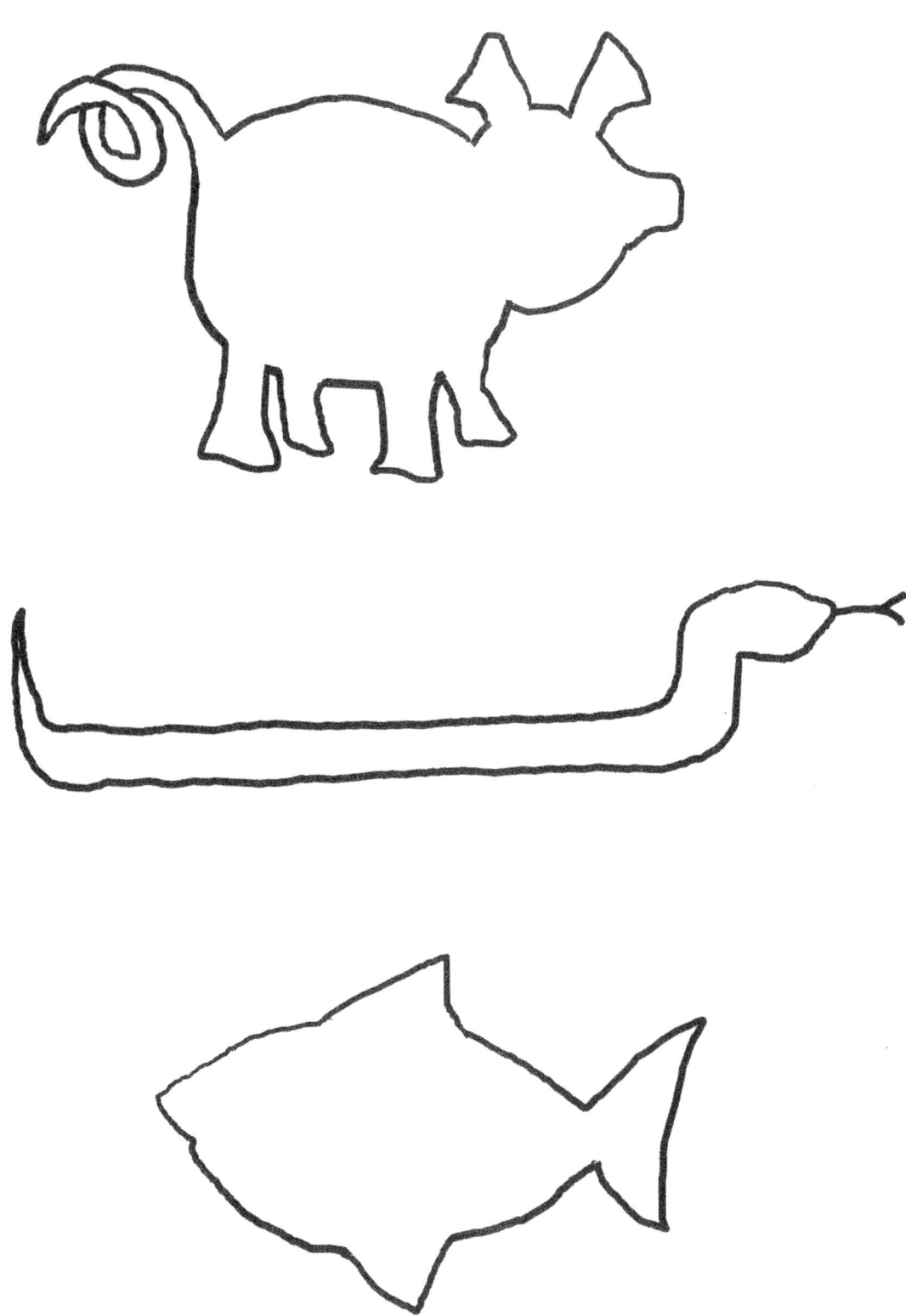

Ghouls are creepy, humanlike creatures. Here are some things to include when you draw a ghoul.

A bald head, or a head covered with wild hair

Dark, deep-set eyes

An unpleasant odor (ghouls don't bathe very often)

Bony, hairy hands

Raggedy clothes

Some people are afraid of the dark. This guy is afraid of the light. . . .

It's **DRACULA!**

Here's Dracula taking a little nap at home.

What do you think Dracula's son is saying to his dad?

Try drawing these Dracula cartoons:

Dracula in a restaurant ordering food. The waitress is shocked by what he is ordering.

Dracula relaxing on the beach. He is protecting himself from the sun in some funny way.

Dracula's son or daughter in school asking the teacher a question that only a vampire would ask.

Aliens

When you draw creatures from other planets, you can make them look like human beings, or you can make them look weird and scary. On the following pages we'll draw different kinds of space creatures. Some will be cool, some will be funny, and some will be creepy. Let's start with space creatures that look mostly like humans.

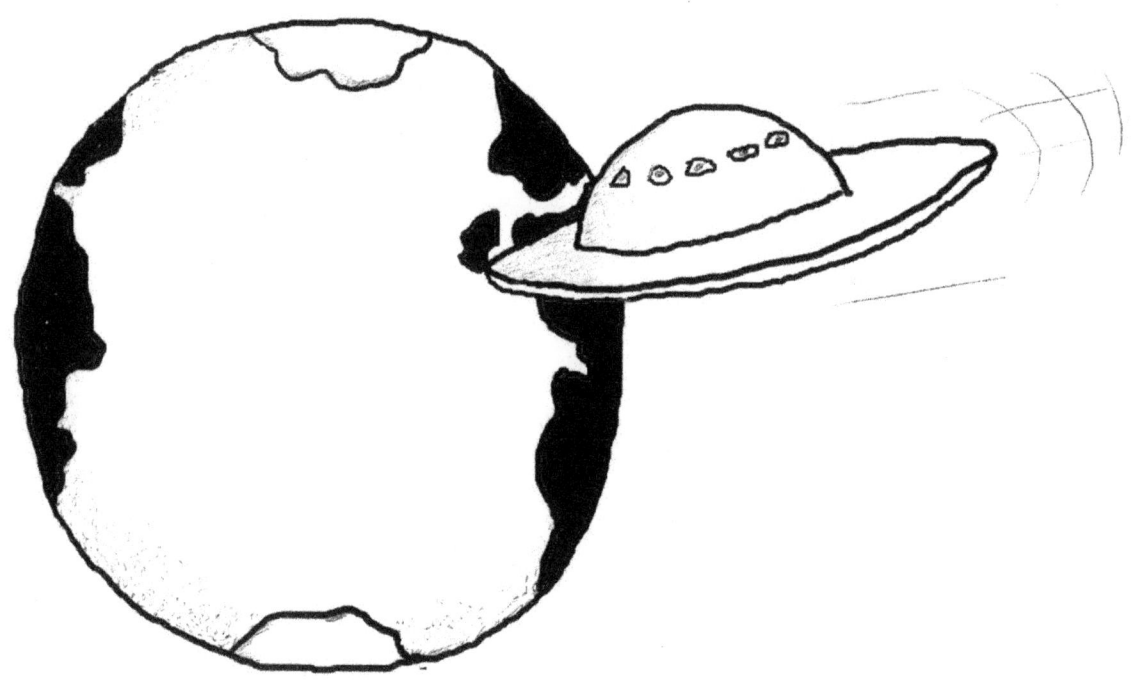

Humanlike aliens often have large heads, probably because we assume that creatures from other planets are much smarter than humans and need the extra room for their massive brains. These kinds of aliens usually have very large eyes, like the character on the left, or little eye slits, like the character on the right. On the next page are step-by-step instructions for drawing these two "brainy" aliens.

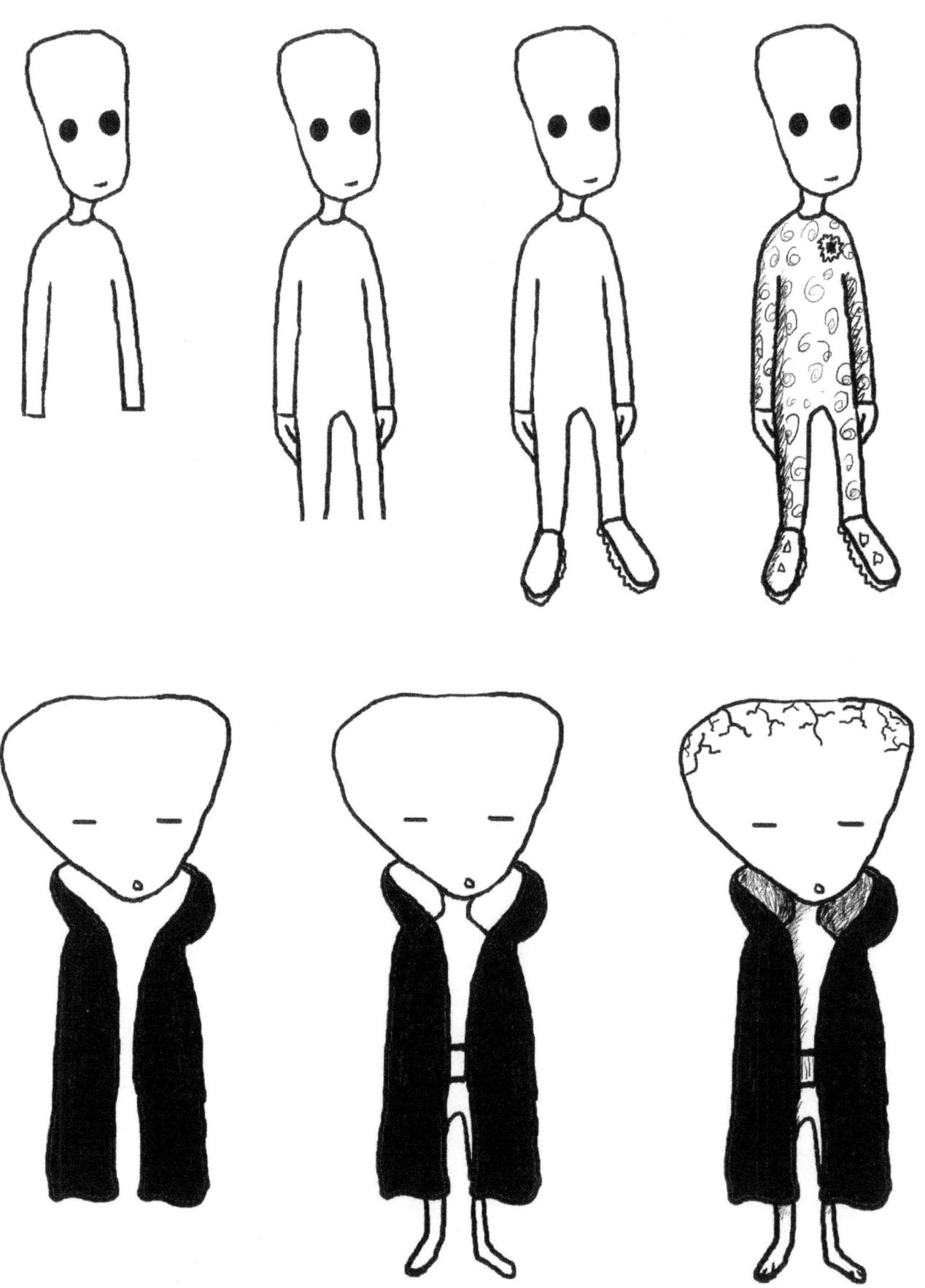

This humanlike alien has hair, ears, arms, legs, a mouth, and a nose . . . everything a human being has. What makes this guy look like an alien is the weird rocket pack on his back and his space helmet.

The proportions of his body are also a little strange. His head is way too big and his arms are way too long.

Alien eyes come in all shapes and sizes. Here are a few that might give you some ideas.

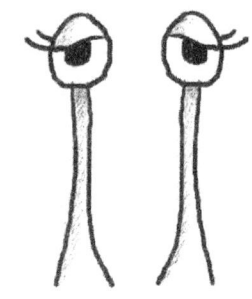

On stalks, like a crab

Oval and flat

Deep-set and dark

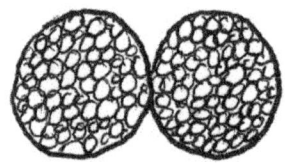

Compound

Pinwheel

Reptile-like

Big, shiny bug eyes

Eyes that are different sizes

You can put your alien's eyes in different places on its body.

On top of the head

On the sides of the head

On the front of the face

All over the head

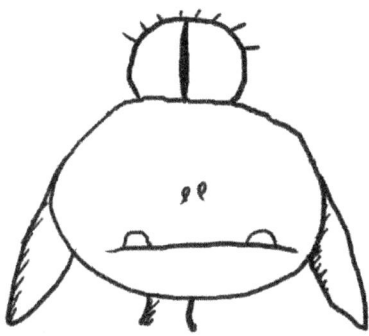

One big eye on top of the head

On another sheet of paper, draw this alien creature several times. Put different kinds of eyes on each drawing. See which eyes you like the best.

It's fun to draw aliens with bodies that look like insects. Many people find insects creepy and disturbing. They're almost like little aliens themselves.

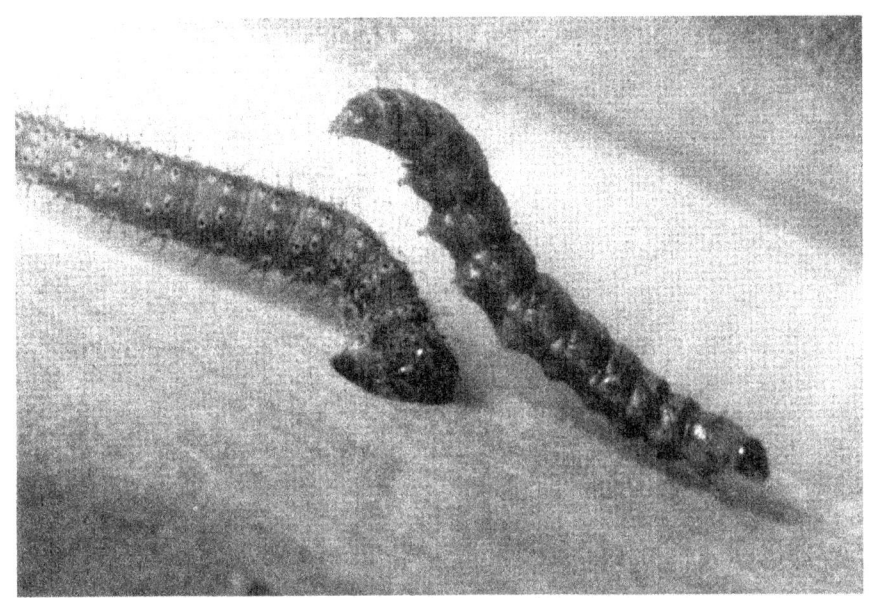

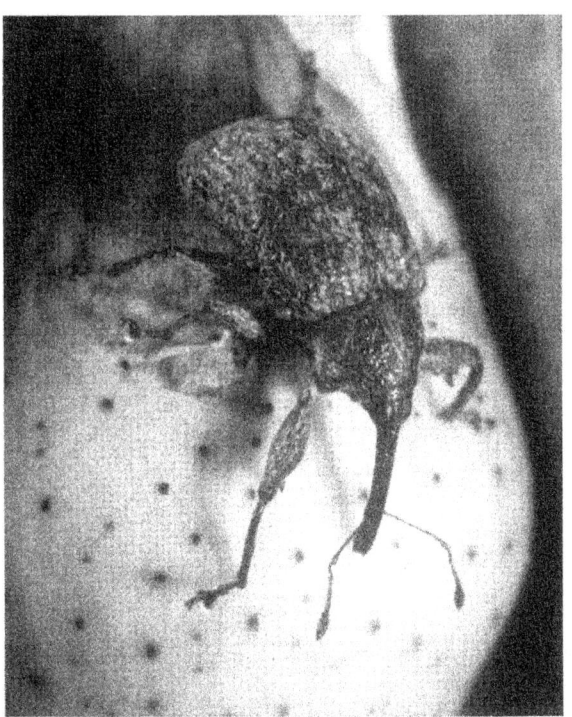

Let's draw some aliens using insect bodies as models.

Basic Insect Bodies

Insects have bodies with three basic parts: the head, the thorax, and the abdomen. The head has the eyes and mouth, the thorax is the part with the insect's wings and legs, and the abdomen contains the insect's breathing holes, digestive system, and reproductive organs.

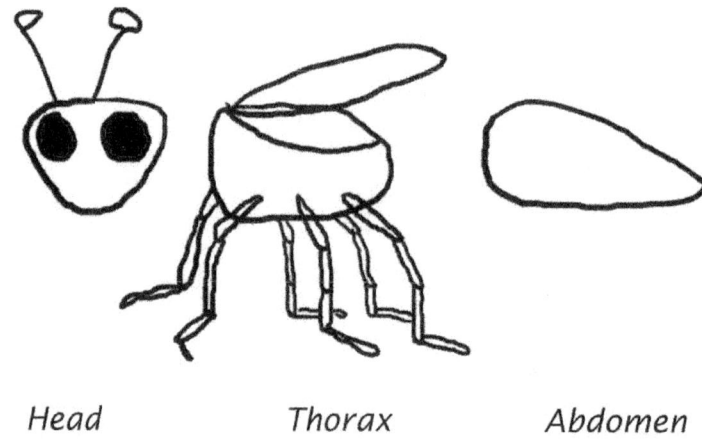

Head   Thorax   Abdomen

By changing the shape, size, and details of each of these body parts, you can create incredibly weird alien creatures.

Remember, we're using insect bodies as models. Real insects always have three body sections, six legs with joints, and two pairs of wings. But that doesn't mean that your aliens have to have the same number of body parts. You can add, change, or remove any body parts you like.

This alien creature has three basic body parts, six legs, and two pairs of wings. But it also has four heads.

This creature also has three body parts, but it has ten legs.

Using the insect body as a starting point, you can connect several basic shapes like the ones below to create the body of your alien.

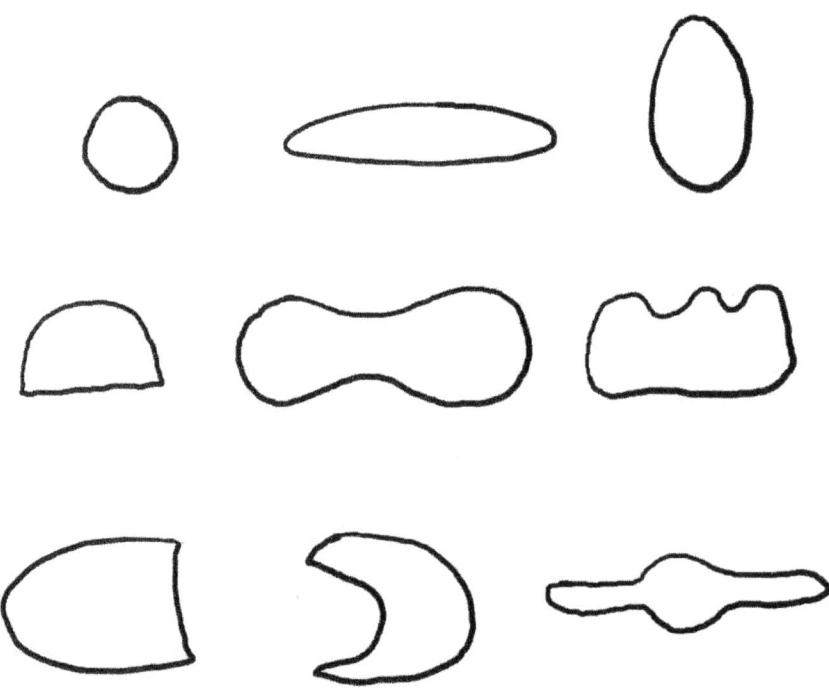

Here's an alien made from these three basic shapes.

On another sheet of paper, connect some of the simple shapes below to create a weird alien creature. Use the basic three-part insect body as a starting point.

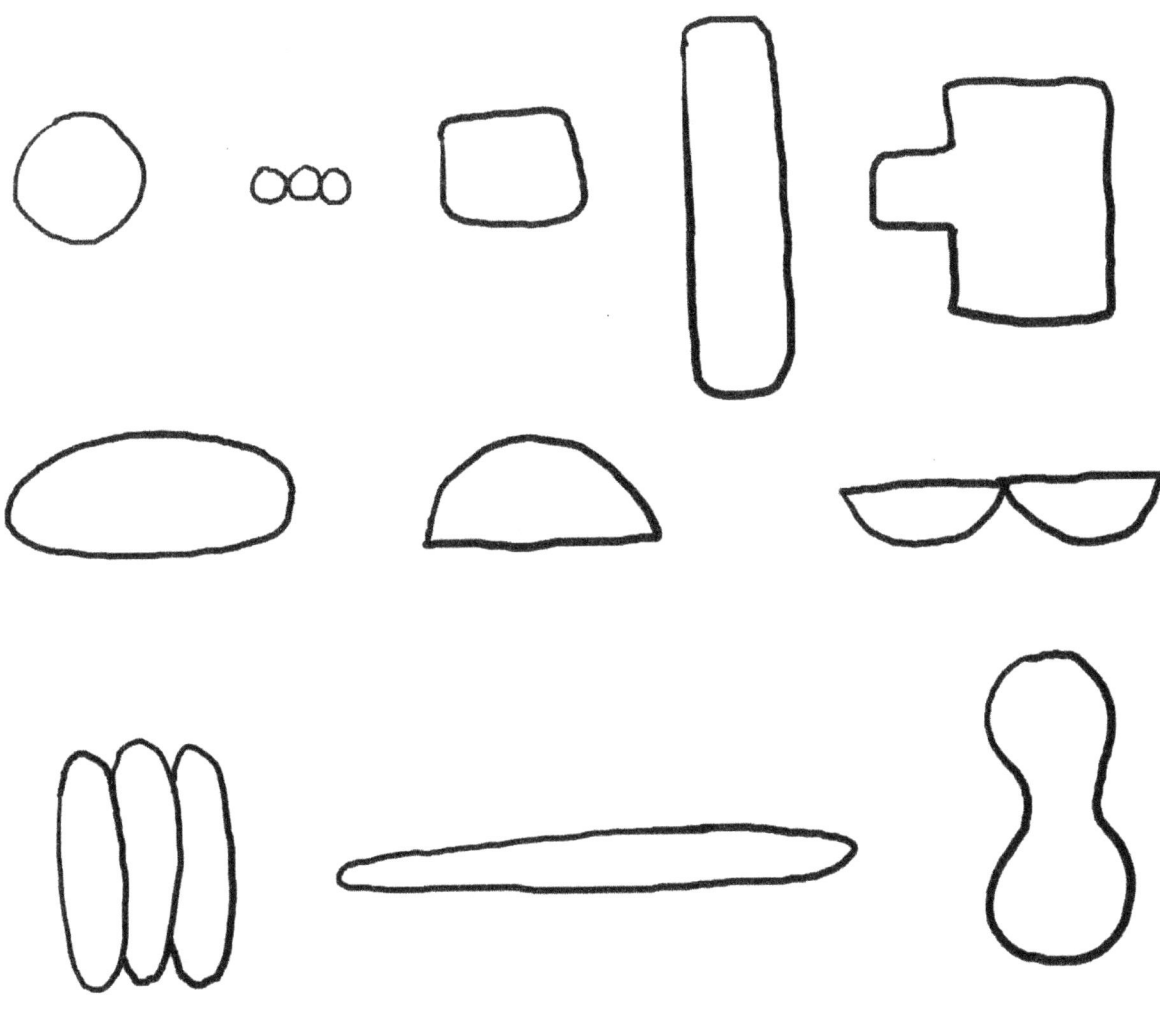

Try repeating shapes, drawing the shapes larger or smaller, or flipping them upside down or sideways. Experiment with the shapes until you have created an alien creature that you are happy with.

Here are some basic rules:

If you want your alien to look dangerous or scary, include one or more SHARP things on it. Here's a good example. This alien creature doesn't look TOO scary.

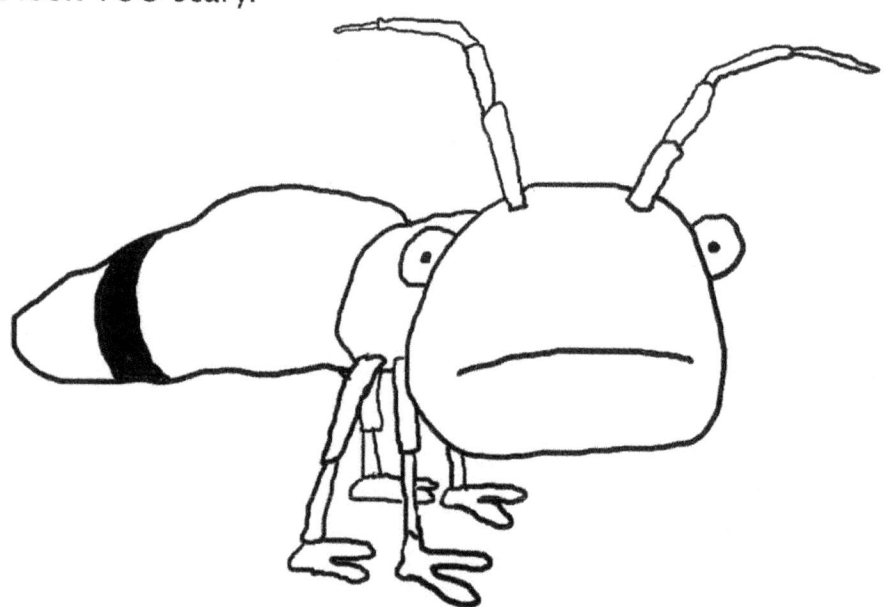

The alien creature below looks MUCH scarier. Why? Because it has sharp, pointy teeth and toes, and spikes on its back. By making things sharp and pointy, we've made our creature look much more dangerous.

Let's draw this alien creature.

Draw the head.

Add a body with a spiky back. Leave a little space on the side of the head for the legs.

Add the legs and the pointy, clawed toes.

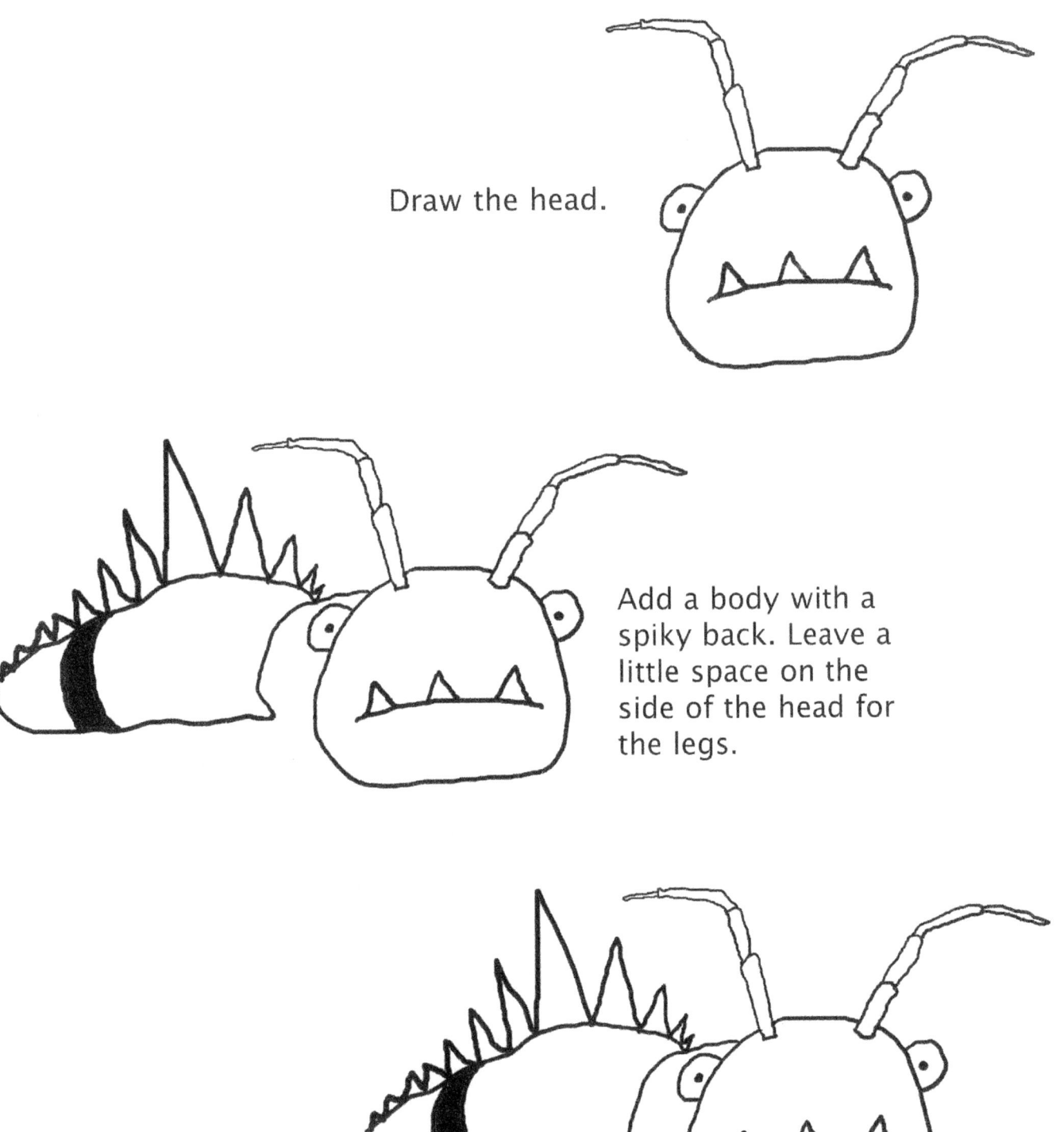

105

Remember: Sharp = scary or dangerous.

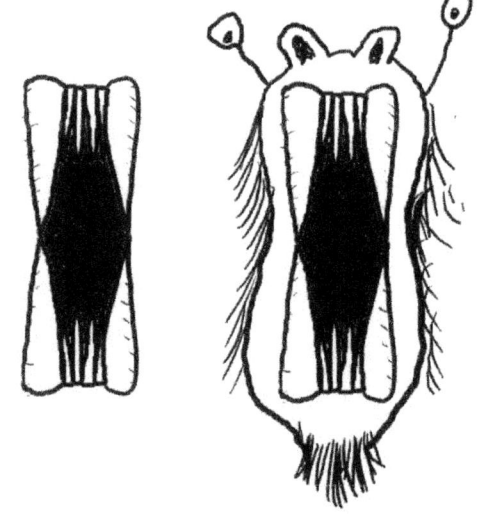

This alien is definitely scary.

Your alien creature doesn't have to have an insect body. You can give it a long, slimy body like a snail or a slug.

Or you can just draw it like a big, wet, smelly blob.

Aliens can even have bodies that look like plants. This alien may have come from a planet where the creatures use sunlight to make their own food, just like plants do on earth. Notice the leaves falling from the alien's body? Maybe he's losing his leaves just like older men lose their hair on earth!

Let's draw this plant alien.

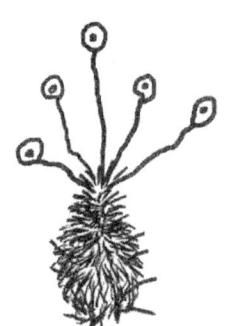
Start by drawing lots of eyes and some fuzzy lines beneath the eyes.

Add a leafy body. Start by drawing the top leaves, then draw parts of leaves underneath. Here's how to draw a basic leaf.

You can also add shading to the leaf.

Now draw some "springy" arms and polka-dot legs and you have a truly weird alien.

Probably the best way to create weird alien creatures is by combining parts of several different species. Check out the creature below. It's drawn from parts of five different animals.

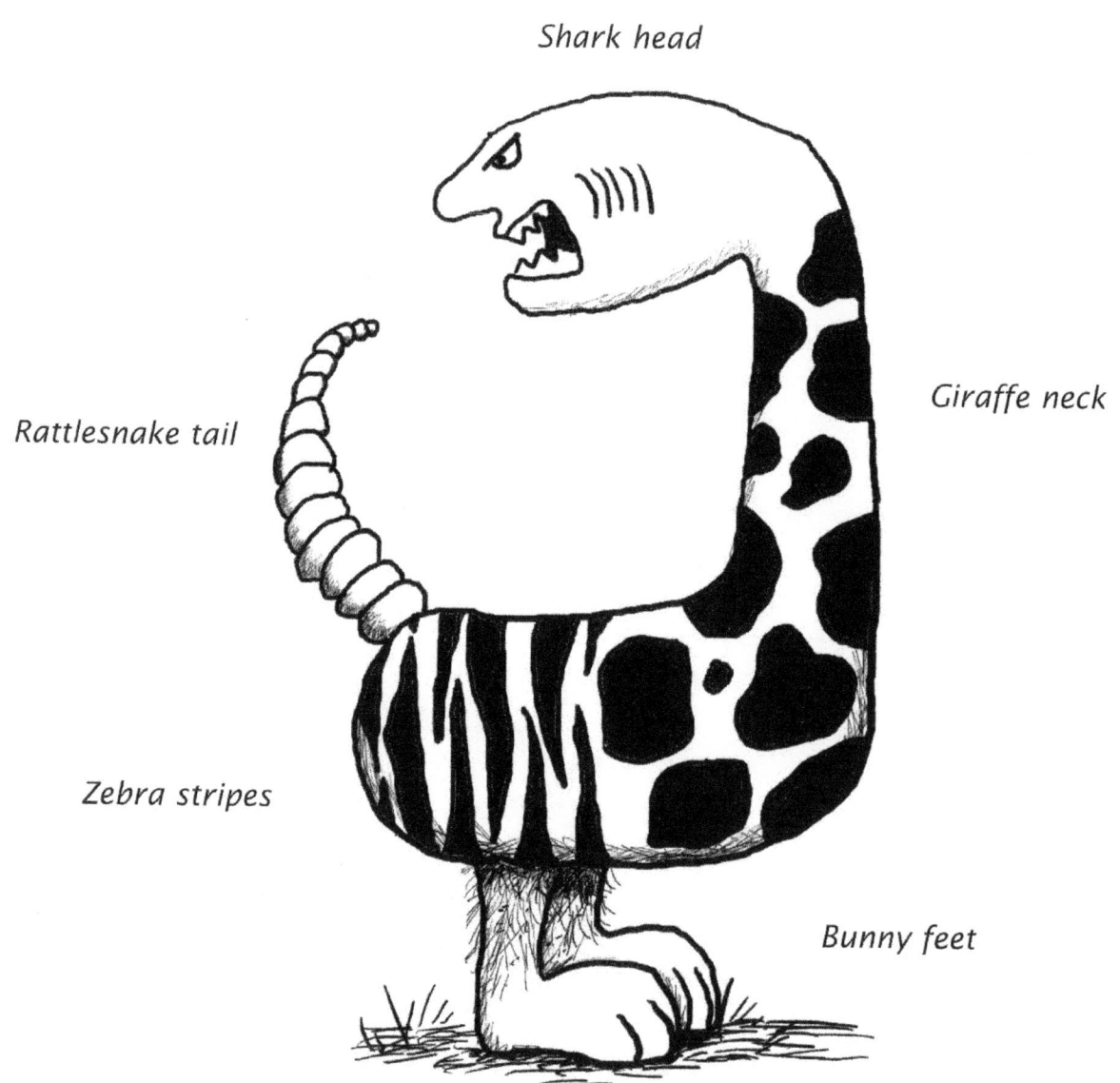

If you think that last creature was weird, check out THIS one!

You can start by taking one body feature each from two different animals and combining them. Here are some examples.

A pig nose plus giraffe eyes

equal the start of a very weird critter.

Rabbit ears plus
cow horns equal . . .

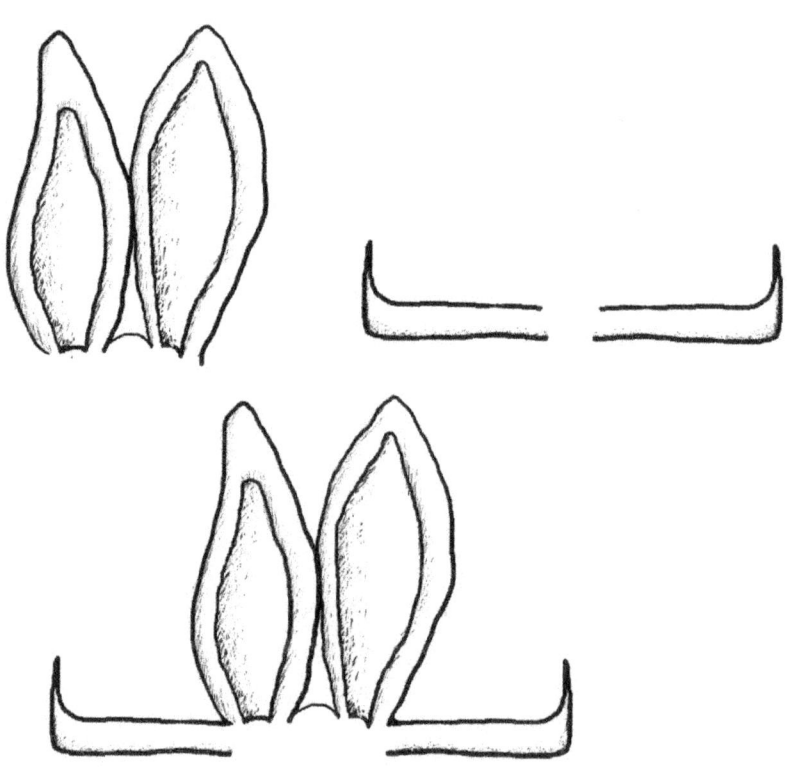

. . . something that's hard to describe.

Here are two animal parts you normally wouldn't see together.

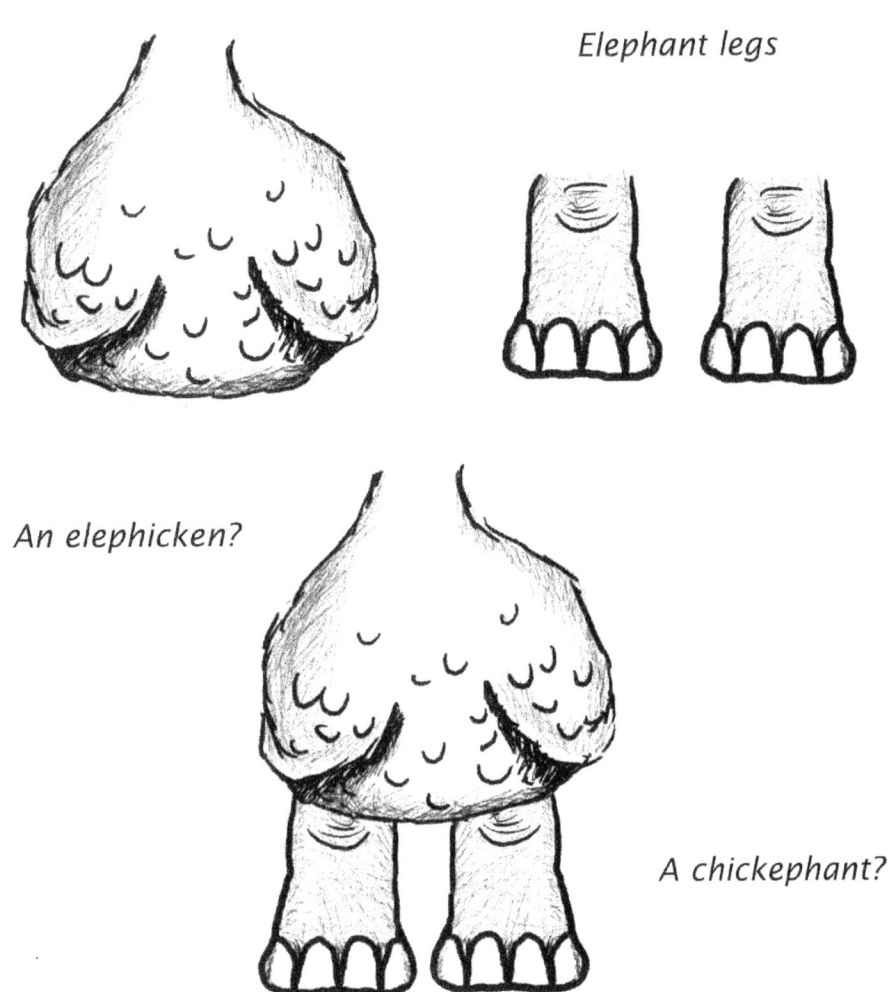

Chicken body

Elephant legs

An elephicken?

A chickephant?

Here are some pictures of animals. Pick one or more body parts from several of the animals and try to create your own weird alien creature.

Alien creatures can also be combinations
of animal parts and machine parts.

By drawing shapes inside of shapes,
you can add lots of details to your aliens.

You can also create weird habitats for your creatures by combining the characteristics of different places on earth. The characteristics of the habitat often determine how the animals that live there look. Some places are rainy, while others are deserts. Some areas of the earth have mountains and valleys, while others have marshes or rain forests. By mixing the characteristics of different places, you can create habitats that could never really exist. Because they're impossible, these places make it easier to imagine the impossible creatures that could live in them.

This weird habitat has cacti growing on a small island in the middle of the ocean during a snowfall. What kind of weird creature would live in a place like this? Look on the next page to find out. . . .

How about a creature with a fish's head, a bear's furry body, and a single, scale-covered leg?

Before you draw your weird creature, try to imagine what characteristics it would need to live in the environment you've created. This creature has a fish's head because it lives in the middle of the ocean. It has a bear's furry body because it needs to keep warm when it snows. And it has a scale-covered leg because it has to walk in the hot sand. See? If you think about it, you can create creatures that fit perfectly into their weird environments.

This environment has large, dry, rocky mountains with two suns and a miniature tropical rain forest. Think about the characteristics a creature would need to live here. If you could design a creature to live in this environment, what would it look like? One possibility is on the next page.

It's lonely on the mountaintop, so the creature might have big ears to listen for other animals. Mountain goat feet could come in handy when this creature climbs the rocky mountain or jumps from peak to peak. At night this creature might use its monkey-like tail to hang from one of the rain forest trees. The sunglasses and long hair would protect the creature's eyes from the double suns. See? It all makes sense . . . sort of.

Certain actions are gross no matter what. On the next few pages you'll learn how to draw aliens doing disgusting things. If you want your aliens to be gross, try adding some of these actions to your alien drawings.

We'll begin with scratching. Scratching can be a sign of irritated skin, or it can be a sign that you have fleas! When you draw hands scratching, it's a good idea to bend every joint of the hand.

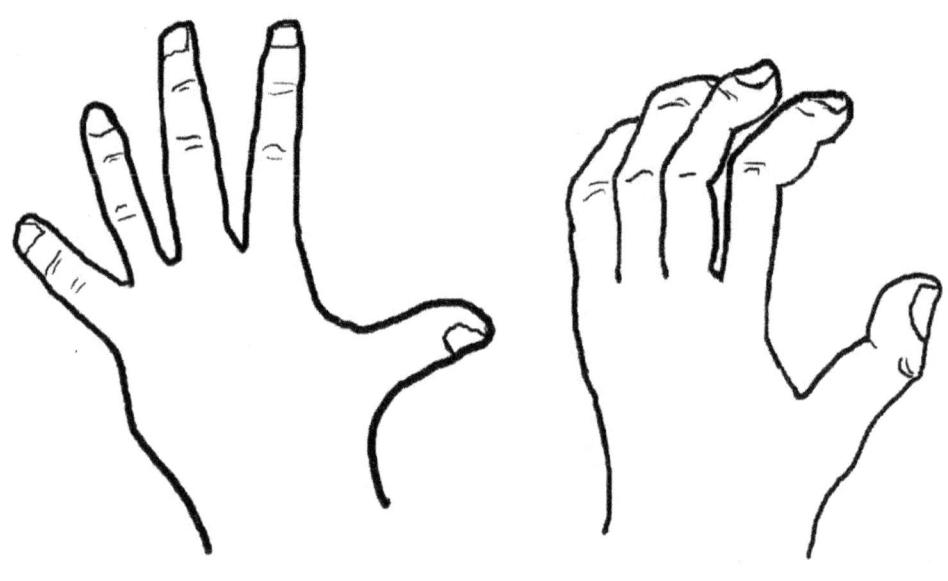

Regular hand   Scratching hand

Notice how the fingers on the scratching hand of this weird alien character are bent at every joint?

When you draw cartoon characters scratching, it's a good idea to draw something falling from the character's skin. Is it dandruff? Fleas? Dirt? It doesn't really matter. It just looks gross and funny.

Drooling is really disgusting, too. Here's how to draw an alien drooling.

First draw a sluglike body and some horns.

Add eyes and a drooly mouth.

Finish by adding some shading on the horns and markings on the body.

Here's a close-up of the mouth. Notice how the drool comes out of the corners of the mouth and gets bigger as it falls. YUCK!

This alien has a body odor problem. It probably smells just fine to other aliens, but to a human nose this guy smells BAD!

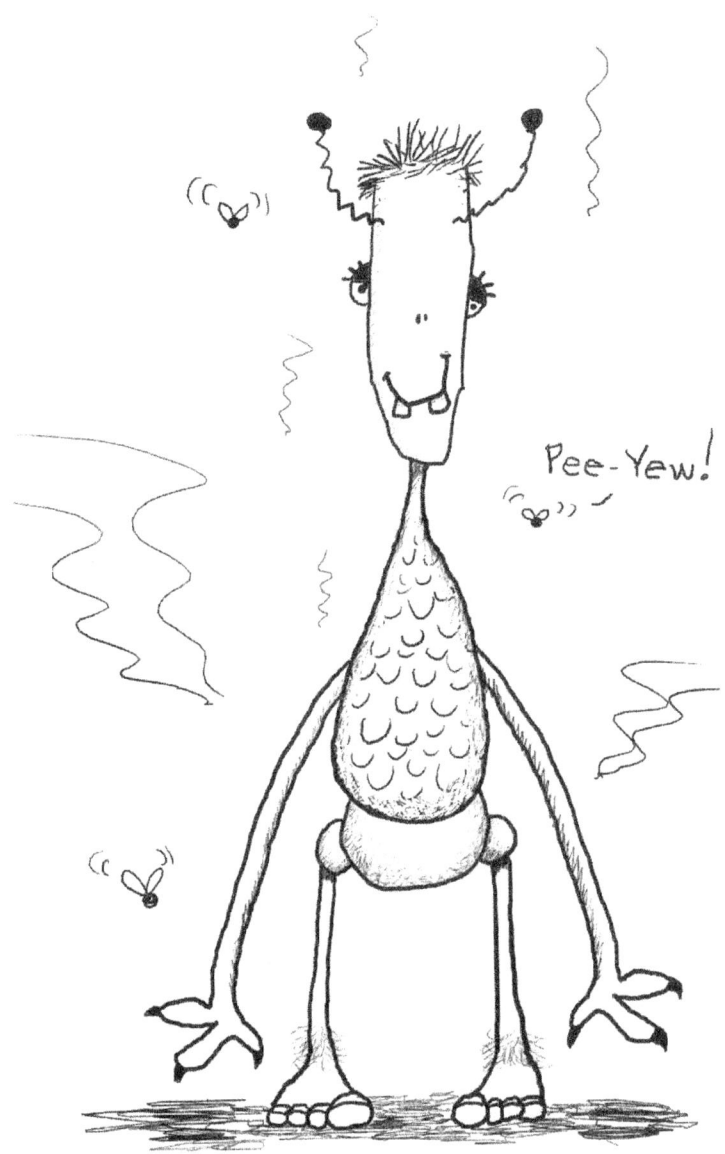

The wavy lines show that there's some kind of smell coming from this alien. The flies show that the smell is unpleasant.

Flies are easy to draw. Begin by drawing a dot, then add little loops for wings. To make your fly look like it's flying, add some "parentheses" near each wing.

Burping makes the burper feel better, but it makes anybody standing nearby feel a lot worse. The trick to drawing a burping person or creature is to stretch the mouth in an unusual way.

If you want a REALLY disgusting alien, try drawing one that scratches, drools, smells bad, and burps all at the same time.

Here are some things you can do with your new cartooning skills:

Create a comic strip featuring your characters and their adventures.

Illustrate your favorite stories or write original stories to go along with your drawings.

Turn your cartoons into personalized greeting cards for birthdays, holidays, or special occasions.

Create a non-fiction "amazing facts book" and illustrate it with your cartoons.

Use your cartoons to decorate the covers of journals, diaries, or notebooks.

Write a tongue twister book or a joke book and illustrate it with your cartoons.

Use your cartoons to create visuals for school projects or presentations.

Make storyboards for homemade videos or animations.

Design trading cards featuring your own original cartoon characters, complete with stats and fun facts.

Let it be known that

_____

has practiced drawing the cartoons

in this book and has learned the

necessary skills to be awarded

the title of

CARTOONIST MAXIMUS

This is an awesome achievement

that entitles the cartoonist

to all the rights and privileges

due someone with this special talent.

OORK!

official seal

Mike Artell
Author — cartoonist

About the Author

Mike Artell has written and illustrated more than forty books and has hosted his own television cartooning show. Each year, Mike visits more than fifty schools and speaks at a dozen conferences, where he shares his techniques for thinking, writing, and drawing funny creatures. Mike also conducts humor and writing workshops for adults.

Complete information about Mike's books, videos and personal appearances can be found on his Web site: www.mikeartell.com.

Index

Aliens, 92-124
    animal combinations as, 110-114, 115, 117, 119
    body odor on, 123
    burping, 124
    doing disgusting things, 120-124
    drooling, 122
    eyes for, 96-98
    humanlike, 93-95
    machine/animal combinations as, 115
    plantlike, 108-109
    with slimy bodies, 107
    weird habitats for, 116-119
Aliens, insectlike, 99-106
    basic insect body parts, 100, 102, 103
    distorting body parts, 101, 102
    scary/dangerous creatures, 104-106
Alligators, 21, 46
Animals. *See also specific animals*
    combining, as aliens, 110-114, 115, 117, 119
    doing opposite of expectations, 51
    doing "people" things, 42-46, 51
    with human emotions, 45-46
    machines combined with, 115
    simplifying, 33-36
Bees, 46
BIG things, 10-17
    giant man, 12-13
    giant turtle, 16-17
    giraffe, 17
    people, 10-13
    thick things and, 11
    whale, 14-15
Body odor, on alien, 123
Body types, 66-69
Burping alien, 124
Cartoons, regular illustrations vs., 8-9
Cats, 42
Cows, 20
Dogs, 26-27
Drooling alien, 122
Elephants, 35-36, 43
Emotions
    animals with human emotions, 45-46
    eyes showing, 49
    mouths showing, 50
Exaggeration, 8-27
    of animal body parts, 20-23
    l-o-o-o-o-ng things, 18-19
    making things BIG. *See* BIG things
    repeating things for, 24-27
    separating illustrations from cartoons, 8-9
    thick things and, 11
Eyes
    alien, 96-98
    people, 30, 49
Fish, 46

Frogs, 23
Gestures, simplifying, 37-40
Giant man, 12-13
Giant turtle, 16-17
Giraffes, 17
Hair, 75-79
Hummingbird, 22
L-o-o-o-ng things, 18-19
Materials needed, 5-6
Monsters
    Dracula, 89-91
    Frankenstein, 81-82
    ghouls, 88
    mummies, 85-87
    Wolfman and family, 83-84
Mouse, 22
Mouths, 31, 49
Noses, 31
Objects, doing "people" things, 47-50, 52
Opposites, drawing, 51-52
Parrots, 33-34
People
    big, oversized, 10-13
    body shapes, 66-69
    doing everyday things, 73-74
    hair, 75-79
    humanlike aliens and, 93-95
    repeating drawings, 24-25
    simplifying, 29-32
    talking, 70-72
People poses, 54-64
    balancing, 63
    exercises, 64
    falling, 62
    sitting, 59
    slipping, 62
    standing, 54-56
    stick men helping draw, 55, 56-63
    stretching/shrinking, 61
    various, 57-58
    walking/running, 60
Pig, 46
Plantlike aliens, 108-109
Repeating things, 24-27
Scary/dangerous creatures, 104-106
Scratching, 120-121
Simplifying, 29-40
    animals, 33-36
    gestures, 37-40
    people, 29-32
Snake, 18-19
Spider, 22
Stick men
    examples, 56-63
    helping draw people positions, 55
Talking people, 70-72
Turtles, 16
Whales, 14-15

www.ingramcontent.com/pod-product-compliance
Lightning Source LLC
Chambersburg PA
CBHW061123170426
43209CB00013B/1655